Corrie ten Boom

WOMEN OF FAITH SERIES

Amy Carmichael
Corrie ten Boom
Florence Nightingale
Gladys Aylward

Isobel Kuhn
Joni
Mary Slessor

MEN OF FAITH SERIES

Andrew Murray
Borden of Yale
Brother Andrew
C. S. Lewis
Charles Colson
Charles Finney
Charles Spurgeon
D. L. Moody
Eric Liddell
George Muller
Hudson Taylor
Jim Elliot

Jonathan Goforth
John Hyde
John Newton
John Paton
John Wesley
Luis Palau
Martin Luther
Oswald Chambers
Samuel Morris
William Booth
William Carey

WOMEN AND MEN OF FAITH

John and Betty Stam
Francis and Edith Schaeffer

OTHER BIOGRAPHIES FROM BETHANY HOUSE

Autobiography of Charles Finney
George MacDonald: Scotland's Beloved Storyteller
Hannah Whitall Smith
Help Me Remember, Help Me Forget (Robert Sadler)
Janette Oke: A Heart for the Prairie
Miracle in the Mirror (Nita Edwards)
Of Whom the World Was Not Worthy (Jakob Kovac family)

Corrie
ten
Boom

BETHANY HOUSE PUBLISHERS

MINNEAPOLIS, MINNESOTA 55438

Corrie ten Boom
Kathleen White

Library of Congress Catalog Card Number 90-56208

ISBN 1-55661-194-3

Originally published in Great Britain by Marshall
Morgan & Scott Publications Ltd.
under the title *Corrie ten Boom*.

Published by Bethany House Publishers
A Ministry of Bethany Fellowship, Inc.
6820 Auto Club Road, Minneapolis, Minnesota 55438

Printed in the United States of America

Contents

1

Looking Back

Tick, tock! Tick, tock! Corrie stirred restlessly in her sleep. The thin, threadbare blanket had slipped off her shoulders. Still unaware of her surroundings, she tugged at it momentarily and sank back into a troubled doze again.

Tick, tock! Tick, tock! The continuous repetition of the noise and a sudden vicious bite from an ever-hungry flea brought Corrie partly back to consciousness again.

At first she was convinced she was back in the old family home at the Beje in Haarlem. Drowsily she listened to what she thought was the regular, busy ticking of the many clocks in her father's workroom. Without opening her eyes she could visualize the high, polished bench over which Father had stooped for so many years, repairing with patience the delicate watches and clocks which were brought to him to mend from all over Holland. Next to Father's was Corrie's own bench and then Hans the apprentice's and by him worked wrinkled old Christoffels.

A smile passed fleetingly over Corrie's lined face. Betsie would be upstairs in the tiny kitchen which led off the dining room. She could almost smell the fragrant aroma of coffee which Betsie had so lovingly prepared for the three of them and the soft new bread awaiting them on the familiar platter in the center of the table.

Crash! A sudden, harsher sound brought Corrie rapidly to her senses. In an instant the cozy vision of the welcoming old house faded and she was keenly aware of her squalid surroundings. The regular, beating noise was just the sound of the freezing rain monotonously dripping through the cracked panes of the dirty window stuffed with filthy rags. And instead of finding herself in one of the spotless rooms in the high, narrow town house in Haarlem, she awoke to face another nightmare day in the hideous death camp of Ravensbruck.

The great tiers of beds stacked three layers high creaked and groaned as the women prisoners stirred to begin the daily struggle against death and starvation. Roll call came at 4:30 a.m. but they were roused by a shrill whistle as early as 4:00. The room was filthy, the bedding rancid and flea-ridden. Whenever anyone moved, a shower of dust and straw fell down on the people sleeping below.

Corrie still vividly remembered the morning of February 28, 1944, when she, together with many other members of her family, had been seized by the Gestapo. After Father ten Boom had died and she had been separated from the rest of her relatives for a while, Corrie had managed to meet up with her sister

Betsie again on a train taking them to the camp at Vught.

But now there was not even Betsie for company—she had died in the prison hospital. Never strong at the best of times, Betsie had become steadily weaker due to the dreadful privations they had suffered together.

During the last few months, Betsie had derived much pleasure and comfort from planning what they would both do after the war. Oblivious of their depressing surroundings, they discussed, even down to the minutest details, the house in which they would nurse people from the concentration camps back to health and strength.

"It's going to be so beautiful Corrie, with gardens all around where they can plant flowers. We'll do it together, Corrie! You and I always together."

After that there was really nothing to keep Corrie going, apart from the well-worn Bible she kept secretly tied in a little bag around her neck and the needs of other people around. Many of their needs were far worse than hers, because they had no hope at all for the future, no Heavenly Father to whom they could pray in their agony and distress.

It was impossible now to visualize the end of the war; without Betsie, Corrie's vision for the future grew very dim and almost disappeared. Would she ever escape from this living hell of suffering? But even in the darkest hour a steady glimmer of faith remained flickering in Corrie's heart.

As far back as Father ten Boom could remember, two strands had been woven into the personality of every member of the family: a sturdy independence and a strong faith in God. Strangely enough, Great-grandfather Gerrit also had undergone the experience of living under a cruel tyrant who had strutted across Europe, invading one country after another. Napoleon, the once insignificant little soldier from Corsica, had overrun Holland with his victorious army and left behind his cruel followers to rule the Dutch nation with oppressive force.

When Corrie had to endure long hours alone in prison after she was first taken captive, she used to think about the family history to while away the time. "Great-grandfather would have understood what we are experiencing today in Holland. Another evil man, Adolf Hitler, is trying to grind all Europe under the jackboots of his soldiers."

One Sunday morning in church, Gerrit and the minister sang a duet from Psalm 21. "The evil one thinks he is free from all bondage, and runs around, while he stirs the people. At the same time, the bad people assume they hold the reins of government. . . ."

The congregation realized it was a pointed reference to their present political situation. It cheered them that someone had the courage to challenge the occupying power. Soon the news of this act of defiance came to the ears of the authorities and Gerrit was saved from jail only because his employer, who was an influential citizen, pleaded on his behalf. He didn't like the thought of existing without the beautiful strawberries which Gerrit grew in the estate hothouses!

So whether gardener or watchmaker, it seemed that the breadwinners of the ten Boom family were perfectionists in their work! Perhaps they were influenced by the text from Ecclesiastes 9:10, "Whatsoever your hand finds to do, do it with all your might." They undoubtedly gained an excellent reputation for themselves in their employment.

But the first male in the next generation certainly wouldn't have made a success of gardening as his father had. He was small and slight in build with crossed eyes. The family moved to Haarlem from the country where Willem started as an apprentice in a watch-repair shop. By 1837 Willem opened his own watch shop in the Bantdjorisstraat and seemed likely to be set on a course of success and prosperity after all.

How was it that the ten Boom family could remember many of the important details of their family life even as far back as Grandfather and Great-grandfather? All too often when an elderly person dies, that particular slice of family history dies with him. Fortunately, long after the war, Corrie's nephew Peter who had been taken to prison with her, found a chest of old family letters and papers. Together they were able to fill in many gaps in their knowledge.

Grandfather Willem's letters to his sister Cato had survived, for instance. After the death of one of his children (eight out of his thirteen children by his first wife died either at birth or in infancy), he wrote, "God has strengthened us during all these events. He is a solid rock in all our need."

Another bitter blow followed when Willem's wife Geertruide also died. But eventually Willem married Elisabeth, who had been housekeeper to the family for two years. The first baby of that marriage was a little boy named Caspar, Corrie's own dear father. He would mean so much to her in later years that she would write a whole book about him, *Father ten Boom—God's Man.*

Fairly early on in Willem's adult life, two important events took place. They were important not only in themselves, but because they colored the whole future of the ten Boom family. Willem became affected by the preaching of Nicolaas Beck, a local revivalist who brought the Gospel to people in a fresh and simple way. As a result, Willem was made one of the founding board members of the Society for Christian Home Visitation. Many organizations sprang up at that time to spread the Gospel and care for the underprivileged.

But the second, even more significant event was sparked off by a simple conversation between Grandfather and his minister, Dominic Witteveen in 1844. Dominic came to visit Willem at his house. "Willem, did you know the Scriptures tell us to pray for the peace of Jerusalem and the blessing of the Jews?"

"Of course I do, Dominic. I've always loved God's ancient people. From them came not only our Bible, but our Savior as well. And are they not His chosen ones?"

Encouraged by this response, Dominic urged Willem to start a prayer fellowship amongst his friends for the Jewish people. It was quite a new venture for Christians in that era because the Jews were scattered all over the world. As yet they had no country of their own or national identity.

However, Holland had given refuge to the Jews ever since the Prince of Orange had driven out the Spanish in the seventeenth century. Amsterdam was even called "the New Jerusalem" by the many Jews who settled there.

Influenced by Isaac Da Costa, a Jew from Portugal who became a Christian, Willem was one of the founder-members of the Society for Israel. Corrie admitted, "Father often told us that love for the Jews was spoon-fed to him from his very youngest years."

This love was to last, and grow, throughout Caspar's long life. One day during the Second World War, when the Nazis had overrun Holland and all Jews were made to wear the yellow Star of David on their clothing, Corrie and her father saw the Gestapo herding Jews on to the back of open lorries. The onlookers had no doubt that the Jews were either being taken off to be exterminated or to forced labor camps.

Corrie felt compassion for these poor people, but her father's reaction was strangely prophetic. "I pity the poor Germans, Corrie. They have touched the apple of God's eye."

So a seemingly insignificant prayer meeting in a watchmaker's shop was to produce amazing results. Exactly a hundred years later, Caspar, four of his children and one grandson were arrested because they were involved in helping to snatch Jews from the occupying German forces.

Corrie summed it up in her writing. " . . . for hiding the Jews, my father, my brother's son, and my sister all died in prison. My brother survived his imprisonment, but died soon afterward. Only Nollie, my older sister, and I came out alive."

This love for God's chosen people, already a family tradition influencing Corrie from her earliest years, was the direct reason Corrie found herself in the death camp at Ravensbruck. She was filthy, desperately hungry and physically and emotionally exhausted.

2

Family History

Father ten Boom was born into the middle of a family of eleven children where he was brought up with few treats and no luxuries at all. Clothes were always made by Mother and passed down in the family until they became too threadbare for further use. At the early age of twelve, young Caspar was made an apprentice in his father's shop. Six years later he left home to start a jewelry store near the Jewish sector of Amsterdam. But before that something very important happened to him.

"When I was confirmed at the age of eighteen, I had already asked Jesus to come into my heart. Before I could partake of the Lord's Supper, I had to make a public confession of my faith. Now that I had found the Lord, or rather, He had found me, I was more interested in spiritual things than before."

Not only was Caspar fully accepted by his Jewish neighbors and included in their important celebrations, he also made life-long friendships with several leaders in a Christian young-men's group he had joined. When he began to work in the Sunday school, he met Cor Luitengh, whom he married in 1884. They settled in a small house in Amsterdam, built in the old traditional Dutch style with a single room on each story and filled with worn-out furniture left to them by Cor's mother.

Although always short of money and possessions, they were very much in love with one another and conscious of God's goodness to them. Three years after their marriage, Father ten Boom wrote to his wife, "What tremendous happiness we have in our children and in all our family. The Lord is so good to us. . . ."

By this time their family was growing and stretching the narrow old house to its limits. For when Betsie, the first child, was born, Mother became ill and had to ask her youngest sister, Anna, to come to help for a few weeks. These few weeks turned into forty long years.

Tante Anna joyfully and wholeheartedly took upon herself all the heavy household chores which became even greater as the family increased. Officially, Father paid her the handsome sum of one guilder every week—but nearly always had to ask for it back to help with the expenses by the middle of the next week. Uncomplaining, she would hand it back, never having spent any of it on herself.

After Betsie came Willem. First teeth, first words, first steps were all faithfully recorded in a book Mother wrote about her children and then presented to them on her twenty-fifth wedding anniversary. How they treasured it!

But not all the anecdotes were happy ones. On New Year's Eve, 1889, Mother wrote in her diary, "It is still so hard to write about our beloved baby, our dear Hendrik Jan, whom we had received from the Lord on September 12, 1886, and whom we had to give back again on March 6, 1889."

Fortunately, the next entry for a New Year's Eve in 1890 tells of " . . . a dear little daughter, Nollie. She is such a darling, with her blue eyes and dark hair, a really intelligent child."

There was to be just one more entry of another birth in the ten Boom family but not before they had moved to a slightly larger house at the very end of the canal. Few customers passed by the isolated shop, and family finances were at their lowest ebb.

Corrie was in a hurry to come into the world. Expected in May, she arrived a month earlier on Good Friday, to everyone's surprise. Uncle Hendrik's verdict was gloomy when he saw her for the first time. "I hope the Lord will quickly take this poor little creature to His home in heaven."

Mother expressed concern in her diary. "The Lord gave us a very little, weak baby—Corrie. Oh, what a poor little thing she was. Nearly dead, she looked bluish white . . . nobody thought she would live."

But like another famous Christian worker, Dr. Barnado, who was laced in a tiny coffin when his life was completely despaired of and yet grew up to be a great blessing to the nation, Corrie confounded all the pessimistic prophecies about her uncertain future. She survived imprisonment in a German concentration camp and thirty years of globe-trotting afterward, preaching the Gospel all over the world. She wrote several books, and reached the grand age of 91 years before going to be with the Lord in 1983.

Father and Mother ten Boom persevered in spite of all the health problems. In those days there were no special baby units with incubators for small, premature infants. In desperation, Tante Anna rolled the baby in her ample apron and kept her tied up in it so little Corrie could gain warmth from Anna's body. It worked. Corrie stopped crying pitifully from the cold.

Even at eight months, Mother anxiously recorded, "None of the other children were so weak. She has to be treated very carefully. During the nights she is quiet, but in the daytime she can have terrible fits of crying." Corrie herself wrote, "Throughout the first year of my life I was a poor, sickly looking creature."

But God has a way of "using the weak things of the world to confound the things that are mighty" (1 Cor. 2:2). Even then He had prepared a plan for Corrie's life through which He would be honored and glorified and many people brought to know and love Him.

After Grandfather died, Caspar was asked to come to Haarlem and work in Grandfather's shop. He rented a small house for the family a short distance away. It was not until five years later that Grandmother left the shop and house for good, making it possible for all the ten Booms to live in the same house as the Lusiners.

Even then it wasn't convenient for them to occupy the old building without a certain amount of alterations.

Father, with the help of an architect friend, drew up plans to remodel the Beje, deciding to make five small rooms on the third floor of the building. In a miraculous way this arrangement made it much easier to hide Jewish refugees during the Second World War. Of course, at the time, the ten Boom family had no idea to what use these rooms would eventually be put, but God was already shaping events to fit in with His divine purposes to save His chosen people. "It was still an impractical house—with steep narrow winding stairs," Corrie wrote. It was, in fact, two houses. The one in front was three stories high, two rooms deep, and only one room wide. Someone had knocked through the rear wall to join it with a thinner, steeper house at the back and a narrow twisting staircase was constructed between them.

Poor Mother longed for a garden but had to make do with pots of flowers on a small area of flat roof. Perhaps this love for growing things was passed on to her daughter Betsie. Betsie always insisted on flowers around the house she planned in her imagination for ex-prisoners of war. "It will do them such good, Corrie, to care for flowers."

3

A Family United

B ut life wasn't always a sad and solemn business for little Corrie. The youngest of a large family circle, she was fussed over and loved by all the others. Corrie called Nollie her "moedertje"—her little mother. As her own mother was always frail and rarely left the house, Nollie would take care of Corrie when they went out for a walk or to play together.

Corrie's favorite toy was a doll called Casperina, named after her dear Papa! But there was little resemblance between them. The doll looked untidy with a cracked head and several fingers missing.

Casperina reflected a bit of Corrie's personality compared to Nollie's doll, which was immaculately dressed just like her mistress. But then, Corrie was never interested in clothes as a small girl. As long as she was able, Mother made most of the family's clothes, but eventually a local dressmaker had to be asked in to help. Corrie hated the "trying on" sessions. Keeping still was torture to her, and whenever she started to fidget she got pricked with pins!

Betsie and Nollie were always more fashion-conscious, and hated many of the drab, dull clothes well-meaning Tante Jans bought them. "Do you think she would mind if I added colored ribbons, or sewed a bit of trimming around the bodice?" Betsie would ask anxiously, not wanting to offend Tante Jans but desperately desiring to look like her other friends at school.

Nollie would sympathize with Betsie, but Corrie never could get worked up about clothing, so many of the unsuitable hats and ugly dresses found their way into her wardrobe. It didn't disturb her in the least!

However, at last a day did arise when Corrie had to face up to a very unwelcome problem.

Life at home was a very cozy existence with so many grown-ups around to give Corrie care and attention. Of course, Mother was often ill and even on her good days the large amount of cooking, washing and cleaning for her extended family kept her extremely busy even with Tante Anna's help.

It was different with Father. Corrie could slip down to the shop and workroom, and if she stayed as still and quiet as a mouse she could watch her father performing intricate repairs on the clocks and watches brought in for him to examine. Each Monday, Father made a trip to Amsterdam to get the correct time from the Naval Observatory. Often Corrie would accompany him, her little hand grasped by his large one. The half-an-hour's train ride looking out of the window at the long canals with their heavily laden barges thrilled her.

Once in Amsterdam, Father would call on wholesalers from whom he bought the spare parts for watches. Sometimes this even involved a little light refreshment for them all with sweet sticky cakes that Corrie loved. But five minutes before noon always saw them back at the station watching for the two movable arms on a shaft at the Naval Observatory to drop, marking the precise moment of 12:00 noon. Father would adjust his own pocket watch, make a few notes with his pad and pencil and then they would travel back on the train again.

Father was a greatly respected citizen in his small town. Once a year he traveled away from home to the Union Horlogeres (Watchmakers' Association) annual meeting in Switzerland, where he was often one of the speakers as a professional watchmaker.

He served on many local boards, one of them being the Rehabilitation Association which looked after the interests of ex-prisoners and their wives and families.

On Sundays there was no work done by the ten Boom family. The only concession Father made was to wind all the watches from his workroom, but he even did that in the living room, to make it different from other days. Twice every day Father reached up for the weighty Bible on its upper shelf and brought it down for a Bible reading around the table. In the morning the workers from the shop joined them before they started their daily work and the children set out for morning school. Sometimes it was a race against time for Willem, Nollie and Betsie to scurry down the stairs and dash across the road to school. It was a more leisurely affair in the evening. After everyone had enjoyed the meal, they exchanged news of the day, and tidbits of information from the shop, from school or about the many activities in which the aunts were involved.

Often there were visitors, and a few more chairs had to be squeezed around the table. Sometimes a little more water had to be added to the soup or stew to make it fill one or two more empty mouths! But however small the amount of money in the family purse, no one was ever turned away or made to feel unwelcome. Mother loved having visitors in spite of the nine members of the family who were always present for meals. Lonely folk were soon brought into the conversation and invited to share in the family musical efforts.

No wonder Corrie felt secure after Father's Bible reading and his nightly visit to tuck her in and give her his blessing before the lights were turned out! It seemed to Corrie that life would always go on like that . . . for ever and ever, without any changes.

But Corrie woke up one morning with a horrible sinking feeling that a very unpleasant change was about to take place. She was old enough to start school. Far from being excited about the prospect, she came down to breakfast with a heavy heart. A sudden brainstorm cheered her up while the others were eating the meal and listening to the usual Bible reading. "I know what I'll suggest—the aunts really need me at home to help them. Father can teach me some arithmetic, and I know how to read already."

Much to her disappointment, no one agreed to her plan. It was a very red-faced Corrie that Father dragged protestingly to school, prying her fingers off the railing to which she was clinging.

But even her howls were drowned by a little boy protesting loudly and being carried into the classroom in his father's arms. As Father kissed Corrie gently, he made her an important promise. "I'll be there at home in the shop when you come back Corrie. And I'll be looking out for you."

So Corrie settled down to the routine of school life with the reassurance that the old warmth and security of home was always awaiting her.

There was still plenty of activity in the Beje even with the four children away for the day. Tante Jans occupied two rooms directly over the shop and workroom and facing the busy street outside. Above her quarters was a narrow attic partitioned off into four tiny rooms with a very sloping ceiling. These were occupied by Tante Bep, Tante Anna, Betsie and Willem.

Tante Anna had joined the family early on, when Betsie was born, but it was several years later before Tante Bep was added to the household. She was Mother's oldest sister and worked as a children's nurse for many years until she became too weak to carry on. Nurses in rich peoples' homes in Holland didn't receive much money or status for their efforts. Rather like Victorian governesses in England, they lived in a sort of no-man's land between the kitchen staff and the master and mistress with their family.

Some days it required all Mother's tact to keep everyone happy in such a small house. Occasionally the aunts would offer their advice on bringing up the children. Tante Bep was particularly prone to this because she compared Mother's children with the children in the last home where Tante Bep had worked. Corrie began to hate the Waller children! According to Tante Bep they were paragons of virtue, tidy, never disobedient or dirty!

Tante Jans had enjoyed several years as the wife of a minister in Rotterdam, helping him in the affairs of the church. When he died, she moved into her two rooms at the Beje fully determined to lead an active and useful life as long as her health was spared. She was always very concerned about her imaginary ailments and tended to pamper herself with special diets and precautions. This did not prevent her from writing poems and Gospel tracts, organizing girls' clubs and even a club for soldiers.

No wonder the children sometimes felt overwhelmed with the many adults in the house taking a close interest in their education and discipline. Fortunately, though, Mother and Father enjoyed such a close relationship that they agreed on everything concerning the children yet still managed to placate and appease the aunts without hurting them or upsetting their feelings. Sometimes it was a very delicate balancing act—almost like walking on a tightrope—between avoiding offending the aunts and reassuring the children!

It worked out in the end in spite of personal faults and feelings, because there was an overwhelming sense of love one for another amongst all the members of the household who were crammed into the Beje.

4

Initial Ministry

*P*eople reading about the grown-up Corrie and her later work for the Lord Jesus might be forgiven for imagining that she was a good, quiet little girl—but that was far from the truth. "I was no angel. Mischief was my middle name," admitted Corrie in one of her books. Her cousin Dot aided and abetted her as they spent many happy hours in imaginative play in the huge empty cathedral of St. Bavo's where Uncle Arnold worked as the verger.

Corrie had become used to school. She played tricks just like the other children and sometimes had great difficulty in wriggling out of a scrape. Once she was very worried that she might be expelled from school after an escapade, so Nollie suggested they follow the example from one of the Psalms that Father had read at the table, "Then they cried to the Lord in their trouble, and He saved them out of their distresses" (Psalm 107). And God really did answer her prayers, after she admitted her wrong.

At the age of twelve, filled with enthusiasm, she

began to write a book, a fantasy adventure about Nollie and some of her friends and cousins. Betsie poured cold water on the whole project by saying, "How foolish! You can't write a book!"

Thoroughly discouraged, Corrie hid the manuscript in a secret cache and when at last she recovered it, the mice had made a good meal of most of the paper!

Still another indication of Corrie's future interests was her struggle to learn English. She couldn't at that stage possibly have any idea of the pattern of events to come. She didn't know that eventually she would make her home in English-speaking America. To help the children with their language studies, the whole family would sit around the table, each with a Bible in a different language. To begin with, each in turn would read John 3:16, (For God so loved the world that He gave His only Son . . .) in his or her particular version.

Most poignant of all, in retrospect, was Betsie stumbling over the words in German. How could they guess then that God was preparing her to use that verse over forty years later to minister to both guards and prisoners in Ravensbruck!

In 1909 came a special celebration of Mother and Father's silver wedding anniversary. As usual, Mother's entry in her diary marked the occasion with thanks to God for all His blessings. Then each child in turn was mentioned, Willem now at the University of Leiden, Betsie the eldest daughter at home, and Nollie training to be a teacher.

"Corrie is now at the Domestic Science School . . . we are very much at peace about her, because we know she is in the Lord's hands and is in the world, but not of the world."

Soon after that Willem left home to become an assistant pastor. He and his wife Tine, whom he married shortly afterward, had a hard struggle to survive with their young family for many years. Eventually, Willem too became passionately involved in the Dutch Society for Israel. His studies at the Jewish Institute in Leipzig, Germany prepared him for the large-scale persecution of the Jews which was to spring from Nazi Germany.

Corrie began her Christian Service in a much humbler way. In great fear and trembling she started telling Bible stories to a class in Sunday school. Betsie gave her a few hints and tips along the way, and quite soon Corrie found herself actually enjoying the experience, unconsciously equipping herself to face up to much larger audiences later in life.

Five months of illness at the age of seventeen kept Corrie at home in bed but fortunately, after an operation for appendicitis, she recovered and was able to enjoy the outside world to the full again!

Like most other teenagers, Corrie developed a longing to taste the world outside the Beje, for experiences away from her own small town and family. After gaining diplomas for her studies in home economics, she felt equipped to take a job as governess to a little girl. Her parents—the Bruins—lived in a large house at Zandvoort about ten miles away from Haarlem and on the seacoast.

It was an eye-opener for Corrie. Anxious to please in her first job, she nevertheless had inner misgivings about life in a very different class of society. There was plenty of space in the huge house after the cramped quarters in the Beje and no shortage of money, yet there was something lacking.

Her weekly trip home to Haarlem for her catechism lessons only served to heighten the contrast. But Corrie stuck at her post until one day Willem arrived at Zandvoort. "Tante Bep has died and Tante Anna is absolutely worn out after nursing her single-handedly for so long. Now she herself needs a good rest," he told Corrie.

Gladly, Corrie went home again with Willem, feeling a little guilty that her release had come only because of Tante Bep's death. But at least she had learned the reason for Tante Bep's difficult personality by putting herself in her aunt's situation. And Willem gently corrected her, "It's not wrong to be happy when a child of God has gone home to her Father," thus helping her to accept the first death which broke the strong circle of the ten Boom family.

Another equally important lesson was to be learned soon afterward. Depressed by a serious fall in trade and her Mother's continuing illness, Corrie blurted out to her father, "Whatever can we do about it all? Everything's so horrible!"

"Just remember, Corrie, that always underneath us are the everlasting arms . . . that makes all the difference."

At the time, perhaps, it didn't make a very deep impression. Years later, however, Corrie recalled the incident and was able to use it to encourage Betsie, lying sick and weak beside her on a dirty mattress in the barracks at Ravensbruck.

In spite of lack of money life was rich and full for Corrie in those years. With Nollie, Betsie and Willem she attended a conference for foreign missions at Lunteren. Visiting there again on her own later, she listened spellbound to Sadhu Singh tell the story of his personal vision of Christ when he was still an unbeliever—rather like Paul on the Damascus Road. Then there were the little Bible talks which Corrie gave in the afternoon at St. Bavo's, sometimes to only a handful of believers.

Corrie enjoyed giving catechism lessons and also teaching Bible studies in non-Christian schools. One important spin-off from this work was her small salary. Corrie saved up for a long time to endow the Beje with two flush toilets—something she had coveted for years! A further luxury item was a bathtub equipped with a gas water heater, a tremendous boon after breaking the ice in hand wash bowls during the winter in their freezing bedrooms.

As always, there was the bitter as well as the sweet to be tasted. Mother suffered a slight stroke through which she grew progressively weaker. In her teens, Corrie went through the emotional ecstasy of first love with Karel, a fellow-student of Willem's, only to find her hopes dashed to the ground later when he was eventually persuaded by his family to marry a girl from a rich, influential family.

When Corrie's heart seemed broken, it was Father in his infinite wisdom who consoled her. "Whenever we cannot love in the old, human way, God can grant us His own perfect way."

Tante Jans was the next member of the family to be called "home." Mercifully, God took away her very real fear of death when her hour came. Many old friends and people she had helped over the years came to her funeral service, telling how she was responsible for bringing them to the Lord.

"It made me think more about time and eternity," commented Corrie simply after the death of her second aunt. Little did she realize then under what harsh circumstances other dear loved ones would have to face death later on.

Another blow struck the family not long afterward. Corrie, talking to Father about business, heard a commotion in the kitchen. Hurrying there, she found Mother slumped against the sink with a large kettle on the floor, the water spilling around.

After lying unconscious for two months, Mother awoke to the world and was spared to them for another three years. Moved to Tante Jans' larger front room from her own tiny bedroom, she could watch people coming and going in the busy street down below. "Corrie," "yes" and "no" were the only words she could utter after her stroke.

One last miracle, however, was granted to Mother. On Nollie and Flip's wedding day, she astonished everyone by singing her favorite hymn at the church service word by word, right through without hesitation. Naturally, the family were optimistic that this sign of hope would herald her recovery, but four weeks later she slipped away in her sleep with a smile on her lips.

A little while before that, however, the Beje was ringing again with the sound of childish voices—and not very happy ones at first. During World War I, Holland had managed to remain neutral throughout the horrendous conflict, but afterward there were many undernourished and deprived people in Germany, suffering because of the long and costly struggle and humiliating defeat.

As chairman of the international watchmakers, Father made arrangements for poor German children to be accepted into the homes of other Dutch members of his profession. When the party arrived, one shy, pale little girl and one bedraggled boy were left with nowhere to go. Clasping their dirty hands in his, Father marched them along briskly to the Beje.

Here Mother was in her element again with small children. Unable to talk and not understanding a word of German, she still managed to soothe and comfort them with a gesture of her hands or a slight nod of her head. Later, Willy and Katy were joined by Mrs. Treckmann and her two daughters Ruth and Martha. When Corrie saw them arrive, tense and weak from the long strain of four years of war and the aftermath of near-starvation, she breathed a silent prayer, "Please, Lord, don't let us go through this in Holland. I couldn't bear to see my own family suffer in this way." It was just as well at that time that Corrie couldn't foresee the future.

Eventually Mrs. Treckmann returned to Germany, but the four children remained. It was some time before they all became obedient, happy children, but with all the love given to their personalities and the food to their bodies, you could hardly recognize the pale, dirty, skinny children who arrived from Berlin frightened and rebellious.

After they had gone back, Corrie lost touch with them for years, but a letter from Ruth, herself now

grown up and married, revealed how she appreciated the love shown to her. Later again, Corrie met
Willy in West Berlin. "It was because I heard people
praying in a house for the first time that long afterward I accepted the Lord Jesus as my Savior. You
planted seeds of love in my heart."

With the children home again in Germany and
shortly after Mother dying, the ten Boom household
resumed its regular pattern of activities. Corrie with
her home economics training assisted Tante Anna in
the kitchen while Betsie was responsible for the
bookkeeping downstairs for Father's business. And
so it might have continued but for the fact that Betsie
became ill in a flu epidemic and Corrie took her
place in the shop.

At first Corrie couldn't find her way through the
maze of figures in the ledgers, yet after some weeks
she began to enjoy her new duties just as Betsie reveled in homemaking, for which she possessed a natural gift. So by mutual consent they changed places
to the benefit of the whole establishment. While
Betsie put colorful touches to the rooms and added
her own special magic to the cheap but appetizing
meals she prepared, Corrie gained mastery over the
untidy columns of figures and went on to train in
Switzerland and became the first licensed woman
watchmaker in Holland. This became the routine of
the ten Boom family for the next twenty years.

However, as Father readily acknowledged,
"Man does not live by bread alone," so after shop
hours and on weekends, Corrie became involved in
many kinds of worthwhile activities. Far from be-
coming embittered over her disappointment with

Karel, she poured out her love and affection on the young people of her home town.

A gap of five years existed in Holland at that time between Sunday school classes, which ended at thirteen years, and YWCA groups for young girls of eighteen or over. As usual, Corrie saw a need there but was reluctant to commit herself because of her inexperience and already very full round of activities.

Talking it over with Betsie, her usual confidante, she was infected by her help and enthusiasm. "Don't worry, Corrie, I'll draw up lists of my old Sunday school pupils and we'll approach them first." Soon the Church Walk Club was started. The girls met at 8:30, going for a walk to the dunes where they played until church at 10 o'clock.

After a while, they also began meeting on Wednesday evenings and walked to Bloemundaal where they were allowed to play games in the gardens and estates of the homes of wealthy people. This further venture was so popular that Corrie and Betsie found they had to recruit additional leaders. This Corrie did by chatting to young women who came into the shop about girls in need and trying to discover if they were committed Christians.

The leaders met once a week to be instructed by Corrie in a Bible story to use for the girls, and to exchange ideas for fresh games. All went well until a rainy August. "We'll have to find a club room!" moaned the leaders in their soaking wet clothes as they waited in vain for the girls on the bridge.

Through prayer they did just that. Later, they extended their activities by renting a gymnastic hall in

Haarlem, full of equipment. But Corrie was always one step ahead. She dropped a bomb amongst the leaders one day by saying, "I want to start a club for boys and girls together." That was unheard of in those days. It would have made prim and proper Tante Jans turn in her grave!

However, Corrie won her point. It was better for fellows and girls to meet together in a club than secretly on the streets. So the Friends' Club began with outings and discussion groups and soon filled a very real need in the community. A young couple, Wim and Fie, started off their married life in the big clubhouse as directors and remained there for many years.

Each evening, when Corrie arrived back home from attending clubs, she poured out her stories— sometimes funny, sometimes pathetic, into the eager ears of Betsie and Father. They were the prayer partners at home, the solid base on which the work was built.

Tante Anna was the last of the four sisters to go home to heaven. Failing for many months, she stayed in bed singing some of the grand old hymns of the church until she grew too weak to use her voice.

After the funeral, the three remaining ten Booms sat around the big oval table. Once it had hardly been big enough for all the people crowded around it. The house, too, had been bursting at the seams with aunts and children. Now several rooms were empty. Would they ever be full again? Who would come to take the vacant places?

5

The Occupation

Corrie need not have worried. Within a very short time she was once again hatching plans to help some more unfortunate children. Miraculously, even while she had just started thinking about it, Willem one day called up the stairs, "Is anyone at home?" Striding up the steep, narrow steps, he announced his errand. "We need a home for the three children of some poor missionaries. Can you help at all?"

After praying about it, Father agreed to house the children. So by the next day the family was doubled to six. Not long after this, they made room for three more girls. Betsie looked after their food and clothing while Corrie saw to their sports and music. One other unhappy little girl, Miep, joined them and soon became content and relaxed in a loving, caring atmosphere. Money was never very plentiful and sometimes thin shoes had to be stuffed with cardboard or newspapers until Father sold an expensive clock and there was enough to buy much-needed shoes and clothes.

Most important of all, the children learned quite naturally about the love of God for each one of them. Years later, after Puck had been imprisoned by the Japanese and treated very cruelly by them, she told Corrie, " . . . when I was beaten . . . I remembered what you had taught me about loving my enemies."

Hans, who lived in a cellar in devastated Rotterdam during the war and even gave birth to her third child there, got in touch with Corrie afterward. "I used to tell my children in the cellar what your father taught us . . . when Jesus takes your hand, He holds you tight and leads you through your life."

As if Corrie hadn't more than enough to do already, she started visiting feeble-minded, mentally disturbed boys and girls and women, telling lonely, hopeless people about the love of the Lord Jesus for them.

Camps and hikes with the clubs in the summer took up even more time. For years the clubs were attached to the Girl Guide Movement but eventually became Netherlands Girls' Clubs. The movement spread beyond Holland to the East and West Indies. SEEK YOUR STRENGTH THROUGH PRAYER was the first article of club law.

So the busy years rolled by. One important change made a profound difference to their lives. Friends gave Father a radio after a long stay in the hospital. Eventually, Father found that he could trust the accuracy of the time signals from Big Ben and save his weekly trips to Amsterdam. Little did they know that this modern invention which brought them so much pleasure with recorded music and talks from all over Europe would prove an essential lifeline in the dark days of the Second World War.

Another red-letter day, a landmark in the history of the ten Boom family, was the hundredth anniversary of the shop—1837-1937. Friends and relatives, town officials and small children thronged the Beje to congratulate Father and consume huge quantities of hot sweet coffee and fresh home-made cakes. Only Willem was missing. When he finally arrived with Tine and their four children, a strange guest was hanging on his arm. The man looked shocking because his face was mutilated.

"He just arrived in Holland today from Germany," Willem explained. "Some teenagers in Munich attacked him and set fire to his beard, because he is a Jew."

Father rose to welcome him eagerly. Here was another of God's chosen people in his home! But a chill somehow settled on the warm-hearted laughter and conversation. Ostrich-like, people tried to dismiss it to the back of their minds, refusing to admit it had any particular significance. "It couldn't happen again," they promised each other. "There will never be another war in Europe in our lifetime—it's only an isolated incident of harassment."

All too soon, however, their half-spoken fears were to be realized. Two short years later Britain, France and Germany were plunged into war. Holland, as before, although appalled by the outbreak of hostilities, was determined to remain neutral. But only a matter of hours after the Prime Minister had broadcast solemn assurances to the nation that there would be no war, Betsie and Corrie woke to the terrifying roar of bombs and a sky ablaze with the red flames of burning buildings. Father slept on but the two sisters knelt in prayer for their Queen and country, and Betsie, incredibly, prayed for the Germans too.

For five long days, the Dutch people held off the Germans but hardly anyone doubted they would shortly be overrun. Corrie wept when she heard over the radio that the Queen had left. Invasion was now inevitable and life would never be the same again.

Surprisingly, real hardship was slow in coming. Yes, there was a 10:00 p.m. curfew, but that was enforced long after the ten Boom family were in bed. Ration cards were issued for essential food supplies, but no one went hungry at first. The German forces ordered all radio sets to be handed in. A family council was held to decide how they should obey this fresh edict. Nephew Peter joined in the discussion. "It will look suspicious, Tante Corrie, if you don't produce one from the whole household. Why don't you take in the small portable and I'll fix the larger one under the stairs over Grandfather's room?"

This made sense to Corrie, so the next day she carried one down to the department store and passed it over the counter to a German official. She was secure in the knowledge that the table model was safe in its hiding place with the floorboards neatly put back in place, looking as though they had never been disturbed. Who would think to investigate under the narrow, twisting stairs of the old house?

Without a pang, Corrie lied quite cheerfully for the first time in her life. "Yes, that's the only one we possess," although afterward she marveled at the ease with which she told this untruth.

Strangely enough, trade was brisker for the first few months of the occupation than it had ever been. German troops with plenty of money in their pockets came in to buy luxury items like expensive clocks and watches to send home to their families.

Father had always been a splendid watchmaker but a very indifferent salesman. To the despair of his daughters he would forget to send in a bill for a long and complicated repair or charge such a small sum it was ridiculous. "But, my dear, it was a privilege to handle such a delicate piece of mechanism," he would reply mildly when Corrie scolded him.

Instead of regarding other watchmakers as rivals and competitors, he went out of his way to be courteous to them and send valuable customers to them if their own trade was slack and poor.

Gradually, however, the ten Booms became more aware of the Occupation. One small incident jerked them out of their complacency. When dogfights were raging one night between English planes and German fighters, Corrie, unable to sleep, eventually slipped downstairs to join Betsie over a cup of hot tea. When she finally returned to her bedroom, she found a ten inch piece of shrapnel on her pillow, sharp and lethal. If she hadn't heard Betsie rattling the cups . . .

"There are no 'ifs' in God's world," said Betsie, with deep conviction.

Another more sinister train of events sickened them even more, although it didn't immediately concern them personally. Father and Corrie on their daily walks noticed signs put up by the Nazis in shops, cafe's and parks, forbidding Jews to enter. Not only Germans were responsible for these, even some of the Dutch people were involved in the oppression of Jews, mainly because by so doing they acquired extra clothes and food coupons. Synagogues were set on fire and all Jews were made to wear the yellow Star of David with its six points on their outer clothing for identification. The sickness that had developed in Nazi Germany was now spreading over the rest of Europe.

Neighbors disappeared. Men, women and children bearing the yellow stars were hustled into trucks by German troops and police. No one knew where they were going or if they would ever return. No one dared to ask.

But that didn't keep people from speculating privately, in the shelter of their own homes. Naturally, the ten Boom family felt very fearful for, and very involved in, the fate of their Jewish brethren after their long association with the Society for Israel. Willem had already given shelter to both German and Dutch Jews in his house and he had valuable contacts with farmers in remote areas, far away from prying eyes.

The first person Corrie and Betsie rescued was an elderly neighbor whose furrier's shop close by had been ransacked by German soldiers. They dashed into the street, "Quick, come with us," Corrie urged him, picking up his spare clothing thrown into the road by the storm-troopers. After seeing him to safety in the shelter of the Beje, Corrie, the fittest member of the family, set off to visit Willem, to ask him to phone the furrier's wife, who was on holiday in Amsterdam, and warn her not to return home.

Having done that, and having the same night sent Mr. Weil safely off into the darkness with her nephew Kik, Corrie heaved a great sigh of relief. Mission accomplished! For a short while, she felt pleased she had outwitted the Germans and that Mr. Weil had escaped from their grasp. But her happiness was short-lived. Of course, it was foolish to think that the problem was solved. There would be more people in even greater distress. Also, by this one act of kindness, Corrie knew she was irrevocably linked with the underground movement—and she wasn't sure what that involved. Would she be called upon to commit deeds that would be hateful to God? How could she act against her conscience?

Nothing dramatic happened for a while after that. Jewish friends came to call and chat with Father, but only in the evening, after dark. Corrie got into the habit of taking completed watch repairs back to Jewish customers in the suburbs, to save them risking a journey to the busy town center. Just small kindnesses, but very precious to those living in daily fear for their lives.

The middle-aged, the elderly, were only too glad to go along quietly to escape the notice of the powers-that-be, but sometimes it was too much for the young. Many were hot-headed and burning to rid their beloved country of the German invaders. One never to be forgotten day, nephew Peter, playing the church organ, suddenly burst into the loud and triumphant strains of the Dutch national anthem. The entire congregation rose to their feet and joined heartily in the singing.

Elated, but sure that the news would reach the ears of the authorities, the family waited to hear the enemy's reaction. Of course, Peter had to pay dearly for his one act of defiance and was taken away for a few weeks to the federal prison in Amsterdam. Surprisingly, he returned safely to them. But after that he was a marked man, as indeed were all other young men of his age. At any moment they could be snatched by soldiers and sent off to work in munitions factories in Germany, which were desperate for skilled men as their own workers were drafted into the armed services.

One day two German soldiers arrived almost without warning. Peter and his older brother Bob had barely enough time to rush into the kitchen, pull up the trapdoor underneath the table and throw themselves into a small chamber made for such an emergency out of a shallow potato cellar. Their two aunts and sister Cocky quickly threw a large cloth over the table and started setting it for a meal.

When challenged, Cocky, who couldn't bring herself to tell a lie, admitted to the soldiers that the boys were under the table. Taking her literally, the soldiers pulled aside the long cloth but probed no further. They marched out furiously, realizing they had been made to look like fools.

A close call indeed! Corrie was again reminded of the time she had lied in order to keep the radio set and Cocky, a young girl, had told the truth and still saved her brothers. Difficult times . . . and difficult decisions! When would it all end? Would life ever be completely normal again?

Somehow, though, the news spread around the area that the ten Booms were known to have given shelter to a Jew in distress. It wasn't long before an elderly lady knocked on the door, fleeing in fear of the Gestapo, and was welcomed by Betsie and given a spare bed. Within days she was joined by two others.

Anxious as they were to assist Jewish people in any way possible, the ten Booms had to face the fact that they could only hope to be a clearinghouse for the refugees. In the center of the town and near the Gestapo headquarters, their movements would be closely watched. Besides, not only their accommodation was limited but their meager rations just wouldn't stretch for many more meals, however cleverly Betsie juggled with them.

Another trip to visit Willem didn't do much to solve Corrie's pressing problems. Although anxious to help his father and two sisters, Willem was already under suspicion himself.

Back at the Beje, Corrie made a mental list of her requirements: places out in the country for her three "guests," a supply of ration cards (because they were never issued to Jews) and a quantity of identification cards to furnish them with false names and addresses. Wherever could she turn? Who would be willing to possibly risk his life in aiding and abetting her?

It looked as though Corrie had come to a dead end.

6

The Hiding Place

A name suddenly flashed into Corrie's mind—
Fred Koornstra—his mentally handicapped
daughter had attended Corrie's classes! A
clandestine visit to his home and a guarded conversation with him assured Corrie that Fred was willing
to stage a fake hold-up at the food office where he
worked. At the cost of two black eyes and a cut lip
given him by an obliging friend, he was able to bring
the so-called "stolen" cards to the Beje, even under
the gaze of a policeman who was chatting to Father
in the shop.

So far, so good! The hundred cards joined the radio under the stairs in a spot so secret and inacces-
sible that even the self-critical Corrie was forced to
admire her own handiwork. No one could guess
what lay inside, she told herself.

Yet that was only one problem solved out of several. Corrie worked away quietly contacting people
in many different professions and walks of life, un-
sure what their initial reaction might be but relying

on God to lead her to make the right decisions through prayer.

An unexpected nocturnal trip with nephew Kik took her to a fashionable home across the city where she met a certain "Mr. Smit" who promised to construct a hiding place for her in which to conceal Jewish visitors in the event of a police raid. True to his word, he turned up at the Beje a few days later. When he and his men had finished, no one would have dreamed that a secret room had been constructed by means of a false wall in Corrie's bedroom. The new plaster and paint were streaked with dirt and water.

The only furnishings inside were a mattress and a jug of fresh water. Supplies of vitamins and dried food were always stored there, together with the spare possessions of any "visitor" living in the house. Every night before the "Jewish guests" went to bed, their day clothing had to be stowed away in the little closet.

Once this hiding place was built, Corrie and Betsie were perhaps lulled into a false sense of security. On a visit to an underground leader, however, Corrie was given a rude awakening.

"Presumably you have frequent drills in your house to speed up your guests in case there is a raid?"

"No, I'm afraid not—we haven't even an alarm bell," Corrie had to admit shamefacedly.

"Then I'll send you an electrician straight away," he promised, and he was as good as his word.

The alarm bells were planted strategically around the house, in any room which possessed an outside window; in the dining room and under Corrie's workbench, for instance. The first time they tried it out, there was such pandemonium that soldiers could have heard them down the street! Also odd, tell-tale little signs were left in bedrooms like pipe-ashes or small personal items of jewelry.

An underground worker who was supervising the drill briefed them on the results, "Too noisy, and far too long! You took four minutes exactly. Now you must try hard to get it down to a minute."

After that, safety drills were organized frequently. With stopwatch in hand, Corrie would look on while everyone disappeared into her bedroom as quickly as possible. When all were safely behind the sliding door, Corrie would make a quick check of each room to ensure no traces had been left behind. Were all the mattresses turned over to the "cold" side so that no one could tell that someone had been sleeping on them only minutes before?

Every time, they tried to beat their own record and the delicious reward at the end was a bag of cream puffs, for which Corrie had to deposit precious sugar coupons at the baker's. It helped to keep the atmosphere light-hearted and more like a game instead of an urgent race against discovery and possibly violent death if they were caught.

Father, Betsie and Corrie also worked out delaying tactics to give the refugees a few more valuable seconds to conceal themselves. They would ask a soldier a question, they decided, or stumble on the stairs in front of him—anything to gain precious time.

Another important lifeline was restored to them; the old telephone on the wall that had been silent for three years. The sound of the bell was set as low as possible so very few people could hear it, but it was essential if Corrie had to keep in touch with other underground workers.

"Visitors" came and went as soon as arrangements could be made. The days seemed long for those who were confined in the house, especially the men who longed for the physical activity which was denied them. Betsie and Corrie tried to compensate by arranging concerts and . sing-alongs in the evening. During the day various refugees took classes in Italian, Hebrew and Astronomy.

One lunchtime found seventeen people squeezed around the table having a meal. Spirits were high and laughter echoed around the room until someone said quietly, "Don't glance behind you. There's someone looking in at the window."

When they realized it was a man cleaning the windows, Eusie, a Jew who seemed likely to stay with them for a long time, had an inspiration. "We mustn't sit here in silence. Let's pretend it's a party and sing 'Happy Birthday, de Opa,' to Father ten Boom."

While they sang lustily, Corrie went outside and discovered the window-cleaner had mistaken them for another house, or at least that was his story. No one could be perfectly sure that he wasn't spying on them.

It seemed as though they had a short period of relief from problems only to move into another crisis. Nollie was taken and kept in the federal prison at

Amsterdam. After seven weeks she was released, probably because Corrie had twice ventured to plead with the prison doctor on her behalf.

God had sent Peter back to them . . . and now Nollie. How good He had been! Shortly afterward, Corrie herself was asked to go to the police station for an interview. Wearing all her warmest clothes and carrying a bag full of vital supplies in case she was imprisoned, she astounded and delighted everyone at the Beje by walking back home the same day after a chat with a guardedly friendly police officer.

There was breathing space again—yet it was like living on the edge of a volcano. But when Jop, a seventeen-year-old apprentice who went out dressed as a girl to warn another underground house that a raid was coming their way, fell into a Gestapo trap, Corrie knew that their days of immunity were almost over. After all, however tried and trusted, Jop was only young and human. What information might he be forced to hand over under torture?

It was only a question of when the Secret Police would come to arrest the ten Booms.

The answer was not long in coming. On the morning of February 28th, 1944, Corrie lay ill in bed with severe influenza. Willem was holding his usual weekly Wednesday service in Tante Jans' room but Corrie was too sick to attend.

She awoke with an unpleasant start as she suddenly became aware of the four Jews who were staying in the house followed by two underground workers desperately racing through her room to get through the secret panel into the hiding place. Ill as she was, she realized it wasn't just another practice and hurriedly threw in behind them her briefcase full of important papers.

Almost immediately a man entered the room and demanded her identity card. She had to dress quickly, pulling on her day clothes over her pajamas. "Where is your secret room?" he demanded.

"I won't tell you," was the firm reply.

"Oh well! It doesn't matter—we'll just leave your Jews there until they starve to death." He smiled cruelly at her.

Downstairs, the rest of the family were assembled. Corrie took off her glasses as ordered. It was just as well because with every question came a sharp blow on the face.

"Lord Jesus, protect me!" she called out, causing the man to sneer at her. But he stopped the beating.

Betsie, too, had received the same treatment. Her face was bruised and bleeding. Meanwhile, the whole house was ransacked and valuables seized. Unfortunately, an unsuspecting messenger from the underground was taken into custody as she called at the door, unaware of the takeover by the Gestapo.

No sooner had that happened than the telephone bell rang. Corrie was forced to answer it with a Gestapo man at her elbow. She dared not tell her friends what was happening but something in the tone of her voice must have warned them and the line went dead.

Betsie handed out a few slices of bread but Corrie felt too ill to eat. The only comfort they all gained was by looking at the text on the wall, "Jesus is Victor." It was hard to believe at that moment, for it seemed as though the enemy had overwhelmed them. As they left the Beje together, Father adjusted the weights of the old clock in the hall. *Who will look after it when we have gone?* thought Corrie anxiously.

Ordering two policemen to guard the house, the Gestapo marched the rest down the road to the police station. As the hours wore on, a large mattress was placed on the floor for them to sleep on. Father, his four children and one grandson shared it. But before they huddled together uncomfortably for the night, Willem, at Father's request read Psalm 91 to them. "You are my hiding place and my shield; I hope in Your word . . . Hold me up, and I shall be safe." Then Father prayed and they slept, Corrie intermittently because she was racked with pain from her sore chest and back. At least, though, they were still together.

By noon the next day they were all taken by bus to The Hague, to the Gestapo headquarters for the whole of Holland. The sight of Father, old and frail, roused pity even in the heart of the chief interrogator. "I'll send you home, old chap, if you'll just give me your word you won't harbor Jews anymore."

What a chance for Father! Would he seize the opportunity to return to the comfort of his own home instead of suffering privation in prison? Father's answer was clear and direct, "If I'm set free today, I shall open my home again tomorrow to anyone in need."

After that there was no more room for pity. Questioning went on for hours and then they were transported by car to the prison at Scheveningen. For a while the prisoners were made to stand facing the wall, although Father was given a chair. As the women were marched off, Corrie managed to kiss his forehead hastily. "The Lord be with you," she whispered earnestly. "And with you," came the familiar reply.

The three ten Boom sisters were stripped of their gold wrist-watches. Corrie lost her ring, too. One by one, cell doors clanged behind them, first Betsie, then Nollie and then last of all Corrie. She was thrust into a cell with four others. They made her welcome, offering her bread and water and showing her a rough wooden bed in the corner, although one of them was afraid of her illness.

Corrie was hungry and tired. Very soon she slept, in spite of her influenza. The mattress was so filthy, clouds of dust irritated her sore throat. The door was only opened to take out their night bucket and their dirty washing water. No exercise was permitted. Corrie tried to make friends with the others and think of ways to pass the time but her thoughts kept returning to Father and Betsie. Both were weak and frail. How would they stand up to prison life? Most of all, Corrie longed to know what had happened to the six people crammed together in the hiding place in her room. Had anyone managed to release them?

She longed, too, for the bag full of her own precious personal possessions she had packed at the Beje, in case of an emergency. It contained a Bible, sewing materials and soap. What a difference they would have made to her existence in that dreary cell! Yet, she had not dared to pick it up as she left her room for the last time because it was directly in front of the panel to the secret cupboard. Had she taken it with her, the man's attention would have been drawn to that most vital, tell-tale place. However hard the sacrifice, it had been absolutely necessary to divert the guard's scrutiny from that area of the room.

Only once was Corrie taken out, and then it was to the hospital, but she made full use of the time. While she was waiting to see the doctor, she asked a friendly nurse for a few necessities. Later the nurse smuggled some of them into her pocket, including copies of the four Gospels. How rich Corrie felt then!

It was disappointing two days later to be placed in solitary confinement. Corrie sadly missed her companions as she lay alone on her mattress, disturbed by the pain in her arm and coughing badly. One day the monotony was broken by being allowed to have a bath. On another, a Red Cross parcel awaited Corrie outside her cell door, but, thankful as she was, she missed being able to share the delicious food with other people. For seven whole weeks Corrie viewed the outside world through the iron bars of her cell window.

Why had she been punished in this way? The only improvement from the shared cell was the window, high up on the wall. As she grew stronger, Corrie's eyes were able to focus longer on reading the Scriptures. With a sharpened corset stay she scratched a rough calendar on the wall. She even celebrated her first birthday in prison alone.

Corrie had hoped she might see Betsie at the showers, but it was not to be. One evening, however, when the guards must have been away on other duties, the prisoners called one to another down the row of cells. "I'm Corrie ten Boom, has anyone seen Casper, or Betsie, Nollie or Willem?" Anxiously she kept on shouting, listening to the replies passed from one to another down the corridor.

Rumors of war news flew around, but far more urgent to Corrie was information about her own family. At last it came, "Betsie ten Boom in cell 312 says how God has been good to her." *Praise Him for that message*, exulted Corrie.

"Nollie van Woerden was released over a month ago." *Thank you, Lord, for her freedom!*

"Willem ten Boom has also left the prison."

How much Corrie had to praise God for! Yet there was a strange silence about her father and she hardly dared think about the fate of the six in the hiding place. It wasn't possible to ask anyone about them, she would just have to go on praying and hoping.

The second answer came before the first. Welcome as Nollie's parcel was to her when it came, with a warm sweater, bright towel, food and needles and thread, it was Nollie's unusual style of writing, sloping toward the stamp, that caused Corrie to remove it carefully and hold it up under the dim electric bulb. In tiny, tiny writing she deciphered the exciting message, "All the watches in your closet are safe."

Corrie nearly jumped for joy. "Watches" was the code word they had arranged for the Jews sheltering in the Beje. What a tremendous relief! God had done the impossible again! Eusie and Many and all the others had not been trapped in a living tomb.

Not until the first week in May did Corrie receive her first letter from home. It shot through the food-flap in her door and fell on the floor. Corrie felt desperate to hear news of everyone, yet nervous in case it was bad.

Forcing herself, she tore it open and stared at the contents. "Father survived his arrest by only ten days. He is now at home in Heaven."

Stunned, Corrie rang the emergency bell for the attendant, but the harsh words she uttered made Corrie long to be alone again. How could anyone who was not a believer understand what sort of man Father had been?

Yet within a few days Corrie could scratch on her cell wall, "Not lost but gone before." In her letter home she wrote, "I was upset for a few days, but that is past. How good the Savior is to me. He not only helps carry my burden, He carries me too."

7

Vught

Although Corrie hoped for some change in her monotonous life, she was a little afraid when it came. Up to that time, the only living creatures she had seen apart from the warden were the birds, soaring and wheeling in the small patch of blue sky, and the tiny, busy ants which scuttled across her cell floor.

Lying in bed, ill-clothed, dirty and still far from healthy, she was startled when the door opened and a German officer entered, a sharp contrast to her in his immaculate uniform bedecked with medal ribbons.

"Now I just want you to answer a few questions," he said. Although he spoke almost kindly, Corrie was immediately on her guard. His manner was a cloak to conceal his real intentions—he wanted to probe and discover just how involved she had been with the underground, she decided.

"Are you well enough to come to my room for questioning?" he eventually asked.

"Oh yes!" replied Corrie, even eager to go to the dreaded examination—anything as long as it meant she could leave her dreary cell and have some exercise and even, perhaps, see other prisoners.

But when she actually stepped over the threshold the next day, the old foreboding returned. "Set a watch, O Lord, before my mouth: keep the door of my lips," her silent prayer went up to the Lord.

Considerately, the officer placed more coals on the fire in his room, noticing how cold and sick she looked. Then the questions came, thick and fast. How disappointing! His kindness didn't stem from natural thoughtfulness for her, but was just part of the process to soften her up so she would give away more secrets.

However, when Corrie finally left the room, she felt she had been able to witness to her captor about her living faith in the Lord Jesus. He had scoffed at the idea of her preaching to mentally handicapped people, saying, "What a waste!"

Corrie answered simply, "God's ways are not our ways. He values equally every single human being." At that she was summarily dismissed.

The hearings proceeded—sometimes in the officer's room and even once in the blessed sunlight, out in the prison garden. In the end, it was the officer who was hungrily asking Corrie questions about the Beje, her family and her belief in God. Pushed into the background was the investigation about her underground activities.

"Can you still believe in God," he asked angrily, "even when your father died in Scheveningen?"

"Prisoner ten Boom is dismissed," the officer said firmly to a woman guard when the hearing was completed. He had shared with Corrie his deep concern about his family in Bremen, constantly bombarded by enemy aircraft, yet he would make no firm promise in answer to her plea to see her own sister Betsie, a few rooms down the same prison corridor. Nevertheless, by walking slowly at his express command, she had a fleeting glimpse of Betsie through a half-opened door as she returned to her cell. They had not even exchanged glances; Betsie's head was turned away, oblivious of the fact her sister was so near. Corrie couldn't fail to notice the "extra" touches in Betsie's cell, trying to make it more attractive and welcoming.

"Betsie hasn't lost her instinct for homemaking," exulted Corrie, as she walked back to her own room with an added spring in her step. She hadn't spoken to her sister or made her aware of her presence, but even a short glimpse had been like a tonic.

Yet a more precious treat lay in store for Corrie. A few days later, the cell door opened again. "Come with me," said the German Lieutenant abruptly, "a lawyer has arrived to read your father's will to the family."

Why should he be concerned about that? wondered Corrie to herself. Nevertheless, all the way to his room she hardly dared hope—could it possibly mean she would see the others at last? First, brother Willem's arm around her, then the sight of Betsie, Nollie, Flip and Tine convinced her she couldn't possibly be dreaming. The Lieutenant kept his back to them, considerately.

Willem, looking drawn and haggard, in a low voice tried briefly to fill in the details of Father's death and the fate of the Jews in hiding. Corrie carefully slipped into a little pouch around her neck a whole Bible which Nollie silently pressed into her hand. Then the will was read.

"Lord Jesus, keep this family in your care," Willem committed them in prayer. No one could know then just how this would be answered in the future as they parted, some never to see each other again, but all were refreshed and comforted.

It was much more dramatic the next time Corrie left her cell. "Get dressed. Pack all your belongings," shouted the guards down the corridor.

Frenziedly, Corrie began to obey, frightened she wouldn't be ready in time. But what did it all mean—was the liberation at hand? Where were they going?

Rumors flew around through the little cracks in the walls where the prisoners whispered to one another. All the activity came to something of an anticlimax when they had to wait hours, sitting on their bunks, until the order came to leave their cells.

Packed into vans and buses, they were taken to a small station. On the platform the prisoners milled around waiting to board the train. Corrie scanned the ranks anxiously. Where could Betsie be? Suddenly, a brief glimpse of her sister's red-gold hair among the others provided the clue. Thank you, Lord! After they surged forward to mount the steps at last, incredibly weary and hungry, Corrie found a new strength and joy. Sitting beside her on the carriage seat was Betsie. By wriggling and nudging others out of the way, Corrie had managed to enter by the same door. The long hours flew past as they talked hand in hand to each other about the events of the past few weeks. They had never been parted for so long before!

"Get out, get out," screamed the guards at four o'clock in the morning, tense and jumpy because some prisoners had already escaped on the journey. With glinting gun-barrels pointed threateningly at them under the searchlights, they clambered down from the train in the middle of the wood.

Kicking and shouting, the guards drove the terrified women on through the darkness. "Don't worry, Betsie," urged Corrie as Betsie stumbled along. "I'll take your burden." So Corrie secured the two pillowcases full of their few personal possessions with the belt from her coat and dragged them along with one arm while with the other she tried to support poor Betsie.

Then—another anticlimax! For hours they were left slumped on hard wooden benches without backs, hungry and exhausted. Her head on the table, Corrie enjoyed brief snatches of sleep until at last some food was brought to them. "Thank you, Lord, for bringing us together again—for keeping us in our own country still," she breathed a silent prayer, for she had found out they were at Vught, in a camp constructed for political prisoners.

Within days, Betsie found a young Jewess who needed comforting. "I'm so terribly scared," she told them. In her diary Betsie wrote, "Each day and night we are experiencing thousands of miracles . . . Corrie's lungs fully recovered."

Another entry noted, "Yesterday, many blessings . . . " Corrie, for her part, filled in as many details as possible in her letters home, "Bep and I are well. We are now working together and even sleep next to each other. We have gone through very much, but life, side-by-side, is now very bearable."

Both the sisters wrote frequently, thanking friends and relatives for parcels received and suggesting items they could include in the future— pencils, toilet paper, vaseline, sugar, Betsie's shoes, butter, jam, condensed milk—even cake, tomatoes and hairpins!

Corrie worried constantly over Betsie's health. "Bep is not healthy. Weighs 96 pounds," says one sentence in a letter. Triumphantly, though, twelve days later she reports, "Bep has gained 8 pounds!" In the same letter she comments, "We are in God's training school and learn much. It is ten times better than being in a prison cell."

Life at first was very boring. Until they were registered at the main camp they had to spend all day long sitting on wooden benches at the tables. No parcels or mail were allowed.

Betsie, true to her nature, faced up to the situation. "Obviously the Lord still has work for us to do here." When they finally arrived at the main camp, utterly exhausted after standing and then marching all day, the weather was glorious. By the first Sunday they joined a worship service on the grass.

"It was wonderful to speak to the Lord together!" rejoiced Corrie. She recognized the need, saw the burdens and, regardless of the grim background, became involved with human suffering.

Soon she was organizing discussion groups. Although imprisoned in body, her mind soared free far above the barbed wire and her sordid surroundings.

"Fall in for work," came the order one morning. Corrie was picked as one of the crew to report to the Philips' factory nearby. At first she was afraid, wondering what cruel guards might be in charge of them. Before long she settled down to the daily routine but found the work, measuring glass rods, rather monotonous. Soon she began to experiment with more interesting tasks, having a trained eye for precision jobs.

"I've never seen any other woman prisoner so interested," remarked the foreman in amazement when he saw her fiddling with radio parts one day.

Corrie laughed, "Well, I don't suppose they were watchmakers like me." From that time on, she was given more interesting tasks to perform and the time passed quite quickly. They were even allowed to sit around on the grass outside at lunchtime. What a marvelous change from the rank, fetid air in the solitary cell at Scheveningen! Of course, the food rations were never enough to satisfy them as they toiled on an eleven-hour shift, but at least a few parcels got through which they shared with their roommates.

On any pretext, though, the officers imposed a mail and parcel ban to punish the prisoners—it could be something as unimportant as untidy beds in the barracks. For a while, it didn't matter. In July Corrie wrote home, "Do not worry that we may not have enough food. The Lord takes constant care of us." Yet in August she was worried about Betsie again, "Bep is often hungry, and is at the moment not gaining any weight."

Characteristically, Corrie didn't bother about herself but was always preoccupied with Betsie's health problems, knowing that she had suffered from pernicious anemia for many years. As the mornings and evenings started to grow cooler, she sent home an urgent request for heavy sweaters. Secretly she hoped they might soon be released—she had heard the rumor that they only had to serve a six-months' sentence at Vught, but just in case, she felt the need to prepare for winter. Roll-calls before dawn could be very chilly affairs if they had to stand for long in inadequate clothing.

It was a blessing that Betsie was employed in the sewing-room. The two sisters spent the working day apart but looked forward to the evenings when they could sit together and chat. So many people needed friendship, help and encouragement in the camp! God had placed them exactly where they could minister to very deep and urgent needs.

Not far away lay the men's camp. As the women marched to work they could see the male prisoners standing in lines for the morning roll-call with their heads all closely shaved. Women who had husbands or sons in that compound alternated between joy and despair—joy when they could send a message or smuggle some extra food through, utter despair when batches of the men disappeared. Would they ever see their loved ones again?

On one never to be forgotten day, the women were standing on benches and window-frames, looking through the cruel barbed wire fence and watching lines of men being assembled and then marched off through the gate, out of sight.

"They're being transported to Germany, for sure. Whatever will happen to them there?"

Even then hope was not dead. After the war—and it couldn't be long now for they had heard rumors of the invasion taking place in Normandy—they would somehow meet up again and take up family life where they had left off, they told themselves.

Suddenly, with quick precision, one hundred and eighty shots rang out. After that, there was no point in hoping any more. . . .

How Corrie suffered with them! True, no man of hers was imprisoned at Vught. Father's spirit had already soared free after only a few days at Scheveningen. She could accept that, even thank the Lord for it now that his frail body had been released. Peter and Willem were free also, and she rejoiced for them gladly, never complaining that she and Betsie were left in captivity. But it was impossible to be unmoved by the sufferings of the women around her.

"How I hated being shut up on my own in my solitary cell," mused Corrie. "It's wonderful to be among lots of people again at Vught. Yet in another way it's harder because I'm immediately involved in their problems. So many women come to us to discuss their anxieties!"

Not for one moment would Corrie have it otherwise. "Bear you one another's burdens and so fulfill the Law of Christ" was the creed her father had taught her. She had always tried to live by it. It was doing just this for a few of God's chosen people that had brought the whole family to the notice of the Nazi regime, but she had no regrets.

Occasionally, when the load of human misery was too hard to bear, she would lean on Betsie and draw strength from her physically frail sister, weakened by prison diet and pernicious anemia. Betsie's faith was the sort that transcended the present hideous realities and feasted on visions of the glorious future in store for them.

One fine Sunday afternoon Corrie drew Betsie's attention to marvelous displays of color and cloud patterns in the sky. The whole expanse was a miracle to Corrie after only seeing small squares of it through her cell window for so many weeks.

"Look, Betsie! It's like a bit of heaven!"

"Yes, Corrie, and Father's already there experiencing fullness of joy! One day we shall be allowed to share it with him."

Lastly there were the children. In spite of the poor conditions, they used to run about rosy-cheeked and healthy, a striking contrast to the poor pale little wretches who were shut up in the cells at Vught with their mothers and allowed no freedom and exercise at all. Corrie found them the greatest comfort and release with their light-hearted natural spontaneity in contrast to the sad and weary grownups, and yet in another way it made her grieve terribly that little ones like these were there at all in such a cruel and barbaric atmosphere. It provided a strange paradox—a problem that couldn't be solved. Even the guards appeared more humane when the youngsters approached them, not yet being old enough to understand how much they should be feared.

Yet, in spite of everything, the long hours of work, the cold, discomfort, hunger, lack of privacy and separation from loved ones, it was bearable and even had its compensations. For sometimes, Corrie and Betsie could point lost and lonely ones to the Savior who was their abiding strength and refuge.

How long would it go on? The prisoners constantly asked themselves this question. Surely it couldn't last forever. What would the next phase be like? They didn't have to wait long to find the answer, and when it had arrived they often wished they were back in the old quarters at Vught. They had never imagined how much more cruelly and inhumanely they would be treated in the future.

8

Ravensbruck

M arch! Double-time!"
Desperately Corrie half-carried, half-pushed Betsie with one arm while carrying their few possessions in the other. Past the barbed wire marking the limits of the compound, through the dingy streets of the prison settlement, they marched to the railway sidings.

At gunpoint they were driven into a railroad car. Built for forty, it contained eighty when the doors were slammed shut. Even then several hours passed before the train finally set off. The air was already foul—no provision had been made for sanitation. At first the women fought and struggled to remain alive. Gradually, most of them contrived to sit on the floor, their legs tucked around the person in front.

"Fresh air at last, hurrah!" A woman with a nail managed to make a small hole in the wooden side of the car. Soon others followed her example. A hail of bullets on the roof brought fresh terror and the train came to an abrupt halt for another wearisome wait.

Corrie squeezed Betsie's hand. This time there would be no rejoicing that they were still in their own country. Hour after hour they rattled farther along the tracks into the heart of Germany. For three days and nights the nightmare journey went on. Crusts of dry bread and occasional sips of water were all that were allowed and the women fought over these.

Although she was almost delirious by the time they arrived, the fresh air revived Corrie slightly as they stumbled out of the train at Furstenberg. Their limbs were cramped and aching after being crammed together for so long.

After a short while, Corrie gasped, "I can't go any farther." She collapsed on the grass by a lakeside, but with the help of Betsie and a friend she was pulled to her feet again. Once they entered the gates of the dreaded Ravensbruck, however, they seemed inspired by a new spirit. Five abreast and singing a patriotic song, they marched into the camp, to the amazement of the guards.

Electric fencing with skull and crossbones warning signs ringed the camp. The women made a mad rush to a row of water jets to wash away the filth and stench of the terrible journey. Yelling and screaming at them, the guards directed the women to a large canvas tent with open sides. Thankfully, they sank to the straw-covered ground only to jump up again as they realized the filthy straw was alive with lice and fleas.

Scissors were passed around among the prisoners. Corrie wept as she cut off Betsie's lovely red-gold hair, but there was no other option with so much vermin crawling around. Thankful for the crude protection of the tent, many were upset to be driven out and made to spend the night under the stars, with only a single threadbare blanket for warmth.

Undismayed, Betsie quoted from the Bible before they sank into a troubled doze. "He gives His beloved sleep." Soon, heavy rain began to fall but there was nowhere they could escape to for shelter.

Two long days and nights later found them still outside, this time in a line outside the bathhouse. Gradually, as they gazed at a great heap of clothing, blankets and provisions scattered around, it dawned on the new inmates that they were being robbed of everything they possessed.

"Quick, Betsie! Let's eat those scraps of black bread before they take them from us."

Even then, the worst ordeal lay ahead. Women were forced to strip off their clothing before they entered the shower room. When they came out, they were merely given a thin cotton dress and a pair of wooden shoes, nothing else at all.

"I can't go through with it, Corrie," whispered Betsie urgently.

Horrified, Corrie sent up a pitiful prayer. "Heavenly Father, save Betsie from this, she is so weak already."

When they entered the room, they were told to undress completely before having their hair checked for lice. Betsie was coughing badly after exposure to the damp and cold. Suddenly she reeled. Corrie was given grudging permission by the S.S. guards to take her to the rough toilets inside the showers.

"Lord, please let me keep Betsie's warm underwear, my Bible and the vitamin drops," Corrie prayed in desperation, not knowing how He was going to answer her plea.

Then help came in a most unexpected manner. In one corner of the room, green with slime and crawling with cockroaches, was a spot where they could hide their treasures.

"Quick, Betsie, take off your woolens and give them to me." Betsie obeyed and Corrie rolled the clothing into a bundle with the Bible and the medicine bottle inside. Then, rejoining the other women, they had to submit to the humiliation of stripping before the cruel glances of the S.S. guards. But by this time it wasn't so hurtful. "The Lord's already answered some of our prayers, Betsie," whispered Corrie triumphantly.

Although icy cold, the water from the showers proved refreshing. It was bliss to be rid of the encrusted dirt from the last few days. Quickly they dressed again, this time in the shabby prison dresses with a cross of different colored material sewn on the front and back. Lining up with the others, Corrie prayed again. This time her prayer was calm. The Lord had provided one answer to their needs and she knew He would not fail them now.

"Lord, I need your angels around me to shield me past the guards," she murmured. And indeed, she looked an odd sight with a bundle tucked under her dress in a very obvious lump. Surely the guards would haul her out of the line! The guards searched the woman in front of Corrie, and then Betsie behind her, failing to search Corrie. When the prisoners had to pass the scrutiny of a second line of women guards outside, Corrie got through unscathed.

Reaching Barracks 8, they were able to slip on the long, warm underwear before they joined the three other women who were already stretched out on their filthy mattresses. They tried all sorts of positions to fit into the impossibly small space. Eventually they all landed up lying across the bed with a ragged blanket tucked around them.

Betsie slept peacefully at last. Nollie's warm blue sweater under her thin prison dress brought comfort and relief from the cold and damp. Corrie lay awake a little longer, praising God for this latest miracle. "Thank you, Lord, that our trust in you has not been in vain."

They weren't allowed to rest for long. "All out for roll-call!" came the harsh cry. They had to turn out at four-thirty in the morning, then stand there for an hour. The sight of a food cart tantalized their empty stomachs, but what little was given to them had to be eaten outside. Other roll-calls followed throughout the day, all unnecessary but deliberately planned to wear them down so they would be incapable of rebellion against the harsh treatment.

Barracks 8 was the quarantine block for prisoners newly arrived. Close at hand stood the punishment block. As they paraded for hours in the cold, the women could hear screams and groans from those who were enduring brutal beatings and the cruel lash. How long could they go on like this?

A further indignity was the weekly sick parade. Naked, they were forced to line up in dank, chill corridors in front of the sadistic guards. The only medical examination was by three doctors, one examined the teeth, one the throat and one looked between the fingers. All the stripping served no useful purpose— it was just part of the total degradation of the place.

Corrie felt the suffering and disgrace keenly. All the poor, thin, bony bodies looked so pathetic as they stood in line. Why should they have to suffer this final humiliation?

Then a sudden thought struck her. After all, the Lord had not asked her to endure anything that had not been meted out to Him. *Lord, when they hung You on the cross, they took all Your garments from You. Roman soldiers even cast lots for them while You suffered. If Your holy person was treated in that shameful way, surely I can bear this with Your help.*

After standing for hours at roll-call, perhaps the next most dreaded thing were the long spells of boredom. The women had not yet been given work assignments, and wearisome stretches of inactivity did nothing for their low spirits or their bodies, weakened by an almost starvation diet. Gradually, some sort of daily routine evolved. Betsie with her precious needles and thread began to mend their tattered garments.

Corrie found many unfortunate creatures needing comfort, among them a poor feeble-minded girl, hardly clothed and half-starved. The sick and the elderly aroused pity in her heart, but there was little she could do for them. She longed for the war to be over so she could continue her mission of caring for people who couldn't help themselves.

Very little war news filtered through to them. The fact that all the Hollanders had been sent far away into the heartland of Germany, although hard to bear, was a good sign in itself. It meant that the Allied forces were extending their spearhead of troops farther across Europe. Surely the end of the conflict must be in sight?

Even this period of boredom could be used for some purpose. More and more women crowded around Betsie and Corrie as they read through the Bible that they had managed to smuggle in. As conditions in the camp grew worse, the prisoners clamored to hear more of God's eternal truth. Bible stories came alive with fresh meaning. Each time Corrie replaced the well-worn volume in the little bag around her neck, she thanked God He had allowed her to keep this Book.

"Betsie, I don't know why the others are here, but I'm sure God has a special purpose in keeping us in this place. Think of all the women who are hearing His Word for the first time!"

Prayer became more real to them, too. There were so many burdens to bring to the Lord—vital, urgent, heart-breaking problems. At least the ten Boom sisters had Someone to turn to, a source of power outside themselves. It was never a question of merely asking for their own needs, but bringing to Him all the sorrows and heartbreaks of their sisters in prison. It would have been an intolerable burden to cope with all the heavy load on their own. After all, didn't His Word say, "Cast your burdens on the Lord and He will sustain you?"

Peter, the Big Fisherman, knew something about that, too. "Casting all your cares upon Him, for he cares for you," is how he expressed it in his letter to

Jewish refugees. And there were plenty of instances where Corrie and Betsie would be witnesses of His loving care. The darker the situation, the greater the miracle, they would find out.

At last the long-awaited orders came to move into Barracks 28. All the women were excited. "It's bound to be better than this, being in the main camp. You'll see, it will be cleaner and the beds are sure to be more comfortable," they promised each other. Yet when they arrived, they peered through windows stuffed with filthy rags where some of the panes were missing only to see rooms of indescribable squalor. As they slept together on the narrow lower bunks, some of the women in the upper bunks fell through the broken slats above and landed on them, bringing a shower of rancid straw with them. A stale smell pervaded this building that was to be their home for several months.

In spite of the conditions, there were others who tried to help the weakest and most unfortunate prisoners. One such woman used to toil far into the night and then afterward creep into Corrie's room with hot potatoes she had cooked on the stove as she had gone about her duties. Corrie kept herself awake, waiting for this very special treat.

It was getting colder now as autumn days arrived. For a little while they were made to work outside shoveling sand. Corrie enjoyed the open air and delighted in the wonderful colors of nature displayed in the birds, the lakes, the hills and the trees all around.

Corrie and Betsie were called up to work with the crew in the Siemans' factory. In an unheated room they had to sort screws with fingers too numb to hold them. Later they were forced to push wagons to the station and carry back heavy iron plates to the factory. They both found the work too hard for their weakened bodies. At Vught there had been a chance to rest and relax at times, even lay one's head down on the workbench and snatch a short sleep. But in Ravensbruck there was no let-up. Everyone toiled for eleven long hours every day. How long could they carry on?

Even now, Betsie never allowed herself to despair. "Think, Corrie, of all the good things God has given us since we've been here."

"Such as . . . ?"

Corrie's voice held a note of weariness.

"Oh well, just the fact that we're together, for a start. We could have been parted in different camps, miles apart."

Corrie agreed. She knew Betsie would have found it almost impossible to survive on her own.

"Then, remember, Corrie, He's spared you a copy of the Bible—that's indeed a blessing. Then we can thank Him for the overcrowding because so many more women can gather around to read His Word—don't you see?"

Corrie did, and assented again.

Then Betsie said something outrageous. In fact, Corrie thought she was utterly and completely wrong. "And we can give thanks for the fleas as well, Corrie."

"The fleas, Betsie? They're one of the biggest plagues here. You must be joking!"

"No, I'm not, Corrie. They're all part of God's plan for us here."

But Corrie couldn't agree to this last remark. This time even Betsie had gone too far.

It wasn't until some time later that both of them understood just why the Lord had allowed them to be surrounded by such a plague of fleas. Surely He could have easily removed this irritating trouble from them.

One day Betsie told Corrie triumphantly. "I've found out why the supervisor never comes into our room. It's because of the fleas! She won't come near in case she picks any up! So that gives us the freedom to read the Bible and talk about the Lord to all these women in this huge room without anyone interfering!"

And Corrie had to agree it was just one more instance of "all things working together for good to those that love God"—even if the all things included dirty, horrible, vicious little biting insects! Even such loathsome creatures had proved to be blessings in disguise!

9

Prison Ministry

*I*n spite of all God's provision, Corrie wondered if they had been too premature in thanking God for keeping them together. After the joy of reunion at Vught, Corrie worried that she and Betsie were going to be deprived of each other again.

Corrie feared the worst for Betsie. Never strong, even when she was cherished and protected by everyone at home, Betsie by this time had become weak and emaciated. Long hours of extremely heavy work, coupled with meals of watery soup and bread that kept them barely above starvation level, had taken their toll on her. One morning the two sisters were escorted by a guard to be examined to see if they were fit enough to be sent on a certain transport. Naked, they were made to walk in front of the doctor. Without hesitation, he proclaimed Corrie as sufficiently healthy. Betsie was rejected as being too weak. Her chronic condition was painfully obvious.

Corrie's heart sank. But even then, at the eleventh hour, came her chance to reverse the doctor's decision. Being passed on to a woman doctor for an eye test, Corrie pretended to have difficulty in reading the bottom rows of letters on the chart.

The doctor saw through her little deception. "Are you doing that so you will be rejected?" she asked, not unkindly.

Corrie saw that she could be trusted. "Yes I am, because I'm worried about my sister who's ill and needs my help."

"Leave it to me. I'll try and fix something."

Another appointment was made for the following day, which meant Corrie missed the transport. So far, so good! Yet, no one would accompany her to the hospital to be examined for new glasses. In her dilemma, she returned to pray with Betsie. What would be the outcome of this fresh problem?

Within minutes they understood God's guidance. "Fall in for the knitting detachment," called a guard, harshly. Eagerly the two sisters received their supplies and retired to their barracks to knit, sitting on their bunks, with very little further supervision by the authorities.

"Isn't that marvelous, Betsie? Now we'll be able to read the Bible and talk with the other women more while we're working."

No suitable glasses could be found for Corrie to enable her to do the more exacting work at the Siemans' factory, so she was allowed to stay with the knitting commando indefinitely.

One night she and Betsie were given red cards by a girl clerk, which meant that they were both judged unsuitable for heavy work. It also meant, as they found out the next morning, that if at any time the camp should be overcrowded, they would be gassed. Yet Someone higher than the German authorities held their lives in His hands—indeed He held the whole wide world in His hands—and no power on earth could exterminate His loved ones unless He willed it so.

However difficult the present, however uncertain the future, there was always some reason to hope, some very evident sign that the Lord had not abandoned His own to suffer at Ravensbruck without any support from Him.

Take the miracles of the vitamins, for instance. On entering the main camp for the first time, all medicines had to be handed in. Corrie resigned herself to parting company at last with her special bottle of Davitamon, a liquid vitamin compound. Admittedly, it was only half full, but to the prisoners it seemed worth its weight in gold.

"Here you are," she said reluctantly, putting it down on the table. To her surprise the woman guard handed it back, remarking, "You can keep it as it's only a toilet article."

Needless to say, Corrie was delighted. She didn't only give some daily to Betsie, but handed out a couple of drops to as many as thirty people at a time. This went on for six . . . seven . . . eight weeks, all from the same tiny bottle, the source never drying up. To Corrie it seemed just like the story in the Bible of the widow's jar of oil that lasted right through the famine.

One day, a young Dutch woman who worked in the hospital brought Corrie a bag full of vitamins to hand out to all the women who needed it particularly. "But don't tell anyone I gave it to you—keep it secret."

Corrie was only too glad to agree. Now she could be really generous with such an ample supply. That evening she tried to shake out the usual dose from the little bottle but it had dried up at last. God had provided another source and the bottle was no longer necessary. Didn't the Psalmist say, "They that seek the Lord shall not lack any good thing?" It gave Corrie and Betsie another chance to witness to others around them about God's lovingkindness to them.

Heartened by this fresh evidence of God's care for His own, Corrie and Betsie would lie together on the slatted boards of their bunk bed crowding under a heap of their coats and a blanket, planning for the future. Surely, peace and freedom would eventually be theirs again, and then they could create a home for young people whose lives had been shattered by the war. Perhaps they would start with the Beje for a time, buying a larger property out in the country when funds permitted. There would be a club-house in Haarlem, too, with all the modern conveniences.

This vision seemed so real at times, they momentarily lost sight of the need, squalor and cruelty around them. Dreams for the future helped them to get through the unhappy circumstances of the present.

One day a poor old lady was so ill she was unable to get up for roll-call. The camp police dragged her out of bed and, when she was unable to stand, beat her and left her lying on the floor. Through the day her condition slowly deteriorated. No one arrived to take her to the hospital and at last she died in the barracks with everyone around.

Corrie felt sick at heart. How cruel and unnecessary! Yet she still had one consolation. Only a few days before she had talked to Mrs. Leners about God's love for her. "Christ died on the cross for you at Calvary. You must put your trust in Him."

Although Mrs. Leners had protested that her faith was small, Corrie wouldn't take "no" for an answer. "Ask the Lord to help your unbelief," she insisted, and the old lady accepted the Lord as Savior, in spite of her weakness.

Night roll-calls in the fog and cold took a further toll. The women shuffled their feet silently to restore circulation. Corrie felt in her pockets for scraps of newspaper to slip across her shoulders underneath her thin cotton dress to keep out the damp chill.

Yet there were others far worse off than she—the women prisoners in the guard-house for instance. Their time at camp was spent behind iron bars, but when they were sent out to work they were employed in very heavy tasks—chopping wood, carrying coal and making roads.

Young children in the camp didn't fully understand their situation. One privilege was allowed them in that they didn't have to turn out for roll-call at night, but were allowed to stay sleeping peacefully in their beds in the barracks. Women prisoners in one way were glad to see the little ones playing around; it helped to make the atmosphere more normal. At the same time they understood it was a bad environment for the children. The diet was sparse and inadequate for their growing bodies. Often their mothers were taken away for long spells to do heavy work.

On the whole, most of the women tried to get on with each other. Although from very different backgrounds and circumstances, they realized they were all in the same boat. The rich and the poor, the important and the nobodies all wore the same thin, tattered garments and survived on the same pathetic diet. Sometimes language was a difficulty as they came from many nationalities, but somehow they managed to make themselves understood to one another. If they couldn't communicate much by speech, they could perform little acts of kindness for each other.

Naturally, though, tempers were frayed and nerves tense under prison camp conditions. Now and again fights broke out, sometimes over quite trivial matters—a woman grabbing an extra amount of food or a bedfellow taking up too much space on the narrow bunks. Then voices were raised to screaming pitch and the women began to fight.

At times like these Betsie grew distressed. Reared in a loving family atmosphere, she was unused to loud voices and harsh treatment. She did the only possible thing. "Lord, quiet these poor people in spite of their anger and irritation. Fill us all with Your grace and peace so that this clamor might die down. Your power is greater than their unhappiness."

Almost immediately the furor died down and calm reigned again. Most people were just thankful for the quiet, but Betsie and Corrie knew it was a direct answer to prayer. There were times also when

Betsie seemed oblivious to what was going on around her. Not that she was uncaring, but it appeared as if she was in such close communion with the Lord she didn't become upset by some of the appalling incidents in camp. Corrie marveled at her serenity but was thankful for it.

Corrie found it infuriating to be kept waiting outside the barracks in the cold after roll-call. The barracks might be filthy, squalid and full of lice and fleas but it represented the only shelter they possessed. "Shall I try to escape?" she asked herself in desperation one morning as a snarling guard cracked her whip over the ranks of women who cowered in dread of the cruel lash.

In her heart of hearts she knew it would be no good. The guards kept too close a watch on them. Then her attention was caught by a friend standing next to her in the lines. Mien had only just been discharged from the hospital and was still running a temperature. How on earth would she manage to do the heavy work expected of them, Corrie wondered? It was too much even for anyone who was completely fit.

This later proved to be a back-breaking job. After pushing loads of potatoes some distance along the rails, in pairs they were made to carry heavy baskets of potatoes up a steep hill. The tough Polish woman who was assigned to work with Corrie despised and resented her because she was so slow and weak. But Corrie's feet and ankles had become permanently swollen as a result of the diet and conditions under which they lived. *I know it looks as though I'm not pulling my weight,* she thought to herself, *but I can't*

*explain to her because of her language. She'll just
have to accept it. I'll collapse if I push myself any
harder.*

Worse than the contempt in the Polish woman's
eyes was the laughter and taunting from the guards
as they saw her dragging along her small quantity of
potatoes. "Just look at her!" they taunted, addressing
her as Madam Baroness, inferring that she thought
herself too grand for hard, manual work.

Corrie toiled on through the long day. She took
comfort in the fact that her Savior had been scorned,
spat upon and misunderstood—all for her sake. At
one stage her feet became soaked. Her shoes were
nearly worn out, the soles flapping off. An appeal to
the guards did no good. "Work in your bare feet,
then," was the only advice she was given.

When she reached the barracks at last, Corrie
sank into a sleep of utter weariness and exhaustion.
Yet she awoke feeling so refreshed that she was able
to lead the service that night. "Be strong in the Lord
and the power of His might!" was the text she had
chosen. A difficult subject perhaps under such circumstances, but she felt more than qualified to speak
about it because in a very personal way the Lord's
strength had been made manifest in her extreme
weakness.

In spite of conditions, people still made an effort
to celebrate special occasions. Take Mieke's birthday, for instance. She was only eighteen and spent
most of her time lying on her bunk seriously ill with
tuberculosis. Yet everyone was fond of her and many
people contributed bits of food to make a savory tart
and salad for her party. True, they only consisted of

scraps of bread, beet, onions and potatoes, but the two dishes looked positively festive to the invited guests. Two flowers and some colored paper decorated the table.

Corrie had a hard battle with herself not to covet extra scraps of food or items of thicker clothing that other people possessed. It was a constant struggle as she was nearly always cold and hungry. It was not just for herself that she craved more—Betsie's condition was deteriorating all the time, causing Corrie a great deal of anxiety. Even in the Beje, Betsie had always been delicate. In Ravensbruck, when they were out shoveling sand and Betsie could only manage very small shovelfuls, Corrie had often urgently prayed, "Dear Lord, please don't let them strike Betsie." The women guards towered above them, ready to crack their cruel lashes over the backs of the prisoners they considered were slacking.

"Willy's lost hope altogether—she's in the hospital now!" went a rumor around the camp one day.

"We've got to do something to give her fresh courage to carry on," said Corrie firmly.

"I know, but it's strictly forbidden to visit in the hospital, you know that as well as I do."

In the end, five prisoners walked over, only to find the shutters closed. "Lord please cause the shutters to be opened," was their earnest prayer.

Miraculously, completely unaware of their intention, a guard first drew back the shutters and then a Polish woman opened the window from inside. In spite of being struck once by a guard and made to move on, Corrie managed to hold a hurried conversation with Willy. "Remember that Jesus loves you and He suffered far worse than you to bear the burden of your sin. Keep close to Him and He will help you through this present difficult period."

Corrie carried on speaking like this until Willy called out, "Thank you. You've comforted me and I feel much better now. I can face up to life again." How Corrie's heart danced with joy when she heard these words! It had been worth all the risks she had taken.

Then came another vicious slap for Corrie from the guard as she slammed the shutters closed again. But it was all very worthwhile because they had been able to encourage Willy. Another victory against evil had been won!

Corrie and Betsie found it heartening to hear many of the women in their barracks admitting how their lives had been changed by hearing them speak about the Lord Jesus.

"God guided me even to Ravensbruck so I should have a much closer relationship with Him."

"After I'm set free, my life is going to be completely different. He sent me here for a purpose."

Corrie's heart thrilled as she heard these testimonies—their work had not been completely in vain. At other times she became downcast and heavy as large groups of these women were shipped off on transports to other parts of Germany. What would be their fate?

There was so little time, so many to reach with the message of salvation before they were carried away to almost certain death. However hard she and Betsie tried, in spite of their almost superhuman efforts, it was physically impossible to reach more

than a small number of all the women who passed
through the camp.

10

Going Home

A s the winter wore on, the weather grew colder. It was hard enough for those who were still comparatively well but the sick suffered terribly. If only the ill could have been excused from roll-call! Somehow they managed to get there, leaning on the arm of a friend or even lying on a stretcher. A wait of several hours in the cold could kill them off even before they received any treatment.

One day Betsie's temperature was sufficiently high to allow her to be admitted to the camp hospital. She was extremely thankful. "How good God is to take care of me," she said to Corrie.

A nurse sharply sent Corrie away. She walked off with deep misgivings. How much more suffering could Betsie take? In her anxiety, Corrie climbed through a window the next day to hide until it was safe to creep out and try to catch a glimpse of her sister.

Betsie was sharing a narrow bed with a French

girl who had kicked her unmercifully through the night—so much so that Betsie had fallen on the floor. Even so, Corrie's sister didn't resent it. "I can talk to her about the love of Jesus. It's a marvelous opportunity. God has allowed this."

Corrie didn't share Betsie's optimism. A nurse pushed her out of the doors. "I'll report you if I see you again." Why did God prolong their sufferings? He could easily have caused them to be released a long time ago. Then a sudden pang struck her. How ungrateful and rebellious she was! Hadn't He already proved in countless little ways how much He cared for them?

They only kept Betsie in three days. Her health had improved very little and it was agony for her to turn out for the morning roll-call at the usual time of four-thirty. A kindly old woman offered her a wooden stool to sit on during the long delays.

The other women stamped their feet while they were waiting and whispered items of news along the ranks to keep up their spirits. But it was impossible to know what was truth and what was rumor. Corrie daydreamed about the time when the Queen would return to Holland—Father had prayed for her every day—and then they would all be free.

In cold, hard fact, liberation was much further away than they imagined. It would be several months before Holland was completely free. Sometimes Corrie's imagination soared above the limitation of ordinary time as she thought about their glorious future in Heaven. She tried to pass this on to others in the barracks, to give them a vision of what lay in store for true lovers of the Lord Jesus Christ. In spite of opposition, she also endeavoured to witness to the guards and even noted a change in attitude in some, though there was no evidence they had decided to follow Christ.

Corrie and Betsie were not the only ones to run a Bible study and prayer session. There was a good spirit of unity among the different groups meeting—often the only reason they did not all meet together was the language difficulty.

Sometimes Corrie found herself giving a short memorial service for the dead. It was an all too frequent occurrence as the months wore on. Then, to make matters more difficult, typhus broke out in one of the barracks. That meant the women had to be kept in quarantine for six weeks—a thousand of them altogether with the use of just eight toilets. "Will anyone at all survive from that building?" Corrie wondered sadly.

Although she had been desperately lonely at times in her single cell at Scheveningen, she would have given anything to have an hour or two on her own to get away from the mass of women in her barracks. Betsie, on the other hand, seemed to derive pleasure from being in the company of others. "I am beginning to love the multitude," she remarked to Corrie.

One evening Corrie received a very distinct message from the Lord, "Before the very cold weather sets in, you will be free." She shared this with many of the others at the next Bible study, convinced that it applied to all of them. She couldn't have known then that she alone would be liberated at that stage—

the others would have to wait until the following spring.

Betsie's release, however, was going to come about in a completely different way. There had been a temporary improvement in her condition after her three days in hospital, but it didn't last for long. Never strong at the best of times, she was wasting away under prison conditions.

One morning, as they were preparing to fall in, Corrie noted to her dismay that Betsie's legs were no longer able to move. *At last they'll release her from attending roll-call*, thought Corrie, but although she pleaded with the officer in charge, it was to no avail. "Even the dying have to report," was the verdict.

Betsie would have no talk of death. Not that she had any fear of it but, "We have so many plans to work out together to help people after the war. I shall get better again." Corrie was still anxious, though, as she and Mien carried Betsie out to sit on a small stool in the cold and dark.

By the end of the day Betsie's condition had worsened. All through the night Corrie tried to nurse her on their narrow bunk, but the place was dirty and cold. If only they were back in the Beje with blankets, hot water bottles and soothing drinks!

By the next morning, the guard was forced to excuse Betsie from the parade. "We'll find a stretcher for her and take her to the hospital later," Corrie volunteered. As Betsie lay there patiently, a Polish woman came by and sank to her knees, making the sign of the cross. Perhaps she recognized that someone who had been very near and dear to them was close to death. Corrie accompanied Betsie to the ward to protect her wasted body from the shower of icy sleet that was falling. At least Betsie would be warmer in there and would be able to rest without any taxing of her little remaining strength.

Corrie made valiant efforts to visit her at noon but was not allowed entrance by the vicious nurse even though she produced a pass. Very well, then! Corrie wouldn't be put off. She tiptoed outside and tapped gently on the window directly above Betsie's bed, making sure the nurse was nowhere in sight. They couldn't really communicate but it relieved Corrie's mind just to steal another glimpse of her sister and to know she still recognized her although she was so ill.

No further permission was given to Corrie to visit the hospital again that day, so she had to wait until after roll-call to check up on Betsie's condition. Corrie wasn't too worried because Betsie herself had been so sure she would recover. "She'll pick up gradually with the rest and treatment in the ward," Corrie told herself as she stopped to peer through the window where she had seen Betsie the previous day.

She was so unprepared for what she saw that at first her mind refused to take in the situation. Two nurses were lifting a painfully wasted body on a sheet that they held by the four corners. It couldn't be! But at last Corrie had to acknowledge that it was the body of her sister.

"It's Betsie, she's dead," she cried to herself. How would she herself survive in Ravensbruck any longer without Betsie's companionship and encouragement in the darkest hours?

Yet she made herself enter the squalid room where the dead bodies were laid out without any respect on the floor. She couldn't brace herself to go there immediately, afraid it might prove too upsetting. But when at length she went, what a precious transformation awaited her! All the lines of worry and anxiety seemed to have been erased from Betsie's face. Instead she looked tranquil and almost happy, thankful to be released and full of joy at being ushered into the presence of her Lord.

Corrie was even granted the extra strength to give a short memorial service for her sister that day from 1 Corinthians 15, "O death, where is your sting? O grave, where is your victory? Thanks be to God who gives us the victory through our Lord Jesus Christ."

It might have looked on the surface as though the Germans had won because another Christian Hollander had died. In reality, it was a triumph for the faithful. Christ had called another of His own home to be with Himself.

As Corrie settled down to sleep that night, she knew she would miss her sister. Betsie had not only shared Corrie's narrow bunk for many weeks but had encouraged and helped her through the darkest hours. Even while she was stretching out on the bed, Corrie saw a Russian woman looking around for a place to lay herself down. Lifting the threadbare blanket, Corrie motioned to the woman to take Betsie's empty place. Gratefully, the woman sank down beside her.

Already there was someone who needed her love and care. Corrie was sure there would be others in the future. How many, she couldn't start to guess. She wouldn't have believed it if anyone had told her how vast a mission field waited for her throughout the world.

Right at that time it didn't look likely that Corrie would be physically able to move far from Ravensbruck. Her feet and legs were badly swollen. Another long wait in the cold for a disciplinary roll-call didn't help her condition. From that day several women became ill. Corrie's only comfort was that Betsie had been spared this further ordeal.

One morning, "ten Boom, Cornelia," was called out on the parade. Corrie stepped forward, hobbling painfully. What could they want her for? Perhaps someone had heard about the Bible she always carried. She joined another small group of women as ordered. "Entlarsen" was the one word addressed to them by the officer.

"You are free—released!" Corrie couldn't believe her own ears. An official document, bearing her name and number was thrust into her hand. Across it was stamped, "Certificate of Discharge."

Even then, it didn't mean that Corrie would walk out a free woman. Another humiliating medical examination followed. Corrie stood there naked, shivering in the cold. "Edema" was the doctor's verdict. She wouldn't be allowed to leave the camp until her physical condition improved.

Unfortunately, conditions in the camp hospital were really distressing. Along with the seriously ill prisoners were several patients who had been injured when the train in which they were traveling was bombed.

The shrieks and groans of the patients kept Corrie awake at night. Corrie resolved to do what little she could for them and kept climbing out of her bunk to take bed-pans to those who were too ill to move. "I'll tell them a little about Jesus as well," she promised herself.

Corrie felt overwhelmed by the evil in the place and the danger of infection. Nightly she prayed for the Lord Jesus to protect her, just as she had asked Father ten Boom to comfort her as she lay in bed as a tiny child.

Thick layers of frost coated the hospital windows. Water in the buckets was covered with a layer of ice. Although Corrie was excused from roll-call, she could hear the women outside stamping their feet for an hour and a half in the sub-zero temperatures.

Rumors flew around the camp that Dutch prisoners—both male and female—were suddenly being treated more humanely. *Surely this must have some significance*, Corrie thought. Perhaps it was that the Allied troops had already reached some areas of the Netherlands.

When Corrie returned to the main hospital for a further check, she was told that she was well enough to be released. It was difficult to believe this after her long imprisonment. But after Corrie was dressed in new, warm clothing instead of the thin cotton dress she usually wore, it began to dawn on her that freedom really was just around the corner.

She was even given back her money, gold ring and watch. One treasured possession she deliberately left behind was her Bible. For days Corrie had looked around for someone who would value it and share it with others. In the end she handed it over in its little bag to a young woman from Utrecht.

"You must sign a document before you leave that you have never been physically ill or badly treated at Ravensbruck," an official told her. Corrie did just that—there was no alternative. Some day the truth would emerge, for the time being her main concern was to return home. She could hardly imagine then how many copies of her best-selling books would be distributed throughout the world, describing conditions as they really were in the camp.

Even the short walk to the station taxed Corrie's feeble strength. One foot dragged after the other and she tried to bribe some German girls to carry her bag.

"You Hollanders are weak and spineless," they jeered.

On the way Corrie saw batches of prisoners sent out for hard labor—chopping trees, building roads or unloading potatoes and coal. Although it made her feel sad, the Christmas-card scene all around with snow-laden pines and frozen lakes was startling in its wintry beauty.

The three-day journey that followed brought its own problems, in spite of being the long-desired trip to freedom. To start with, Corrie's meager bread supply was stolen the first day. At one station a kindly Red Cross nurse came to Corrie's rescue. "Swallow this as quickly as you can!" the nurse whispered, pushing a plate of hot soup toward Corrie.

At Uelgen they were not allowed to sleep in the station. Time dragged on. Trains failed to arrive punctually, sometimes not turning up at all. Corrie's legs grew wearier and slower from climbing off one train and on to another over and over again. Would the journey never end?

Before stepping on Dutch soil, Corrie had to pass through many of the ruined cities of Germany. Heaps of rubble marked the spot where once happy homes had flourished. Corrie did not rejoice over the defeat of her enemies, who had done so much to harm her and had been responsible for the death of her father in prison and her sister in a concentration camp. Instead, she was filled with compassion for the poor, unhappy, deluded people of that country. They had sown their crop of cruelty and inhumanity, and now they were reaping the fruits. What an immense amount of human misery could be laid at the door of Adolf Hitler!

It was heartening at one stage of their journey, when there was no food available for travelers at the station, to be driven to a small house outside and treated like human beings again. A kindly woman, assisted by a young girl, served them with coffee and bread and jam. Nothing was too much trouble for them. Corrie felt she had been transported into the Germany of prewar years. How good it was to come in contact with people whose characters had not been changed by the evil Nazi doctrine!

Finally they crossed the border into Holland. Miles and miles of flat fields stretched ahead, but they could not travel far into their own country. Tracks had been torn up by the constant bombing from the air. For the moment, Corrie had come to a full stop in her long journey.

11

The Power of Forgiveness

Arriving in Groningen, Corrie limped painfully
to a hospital not far from the station. Falter-
ingly, she began to give a brief account of her
story to a white-coated nurse who had invited her
into her small office.

When she had listened to Corrie's amazing re-
cital, the nurse left the room. A few minutes later she
returned with a tray—the first tray Corrie had seen
for many months. "Here you are; it isn't very much,
only a cup of tea and a roll, but your stomach isn't
ready for rich food. I haven't even spread any butter
on the roll—it's better like that at first."

How touched Corrie felt at these words! What a
marvelous change it was to be looked after by someone who really cared for her welfare instead of kicking and insulting her!

A further treat was in store for her. An elderly
minister had arrived to give a service on the wards
and Corrie was allowed to join in. She found herself
contrasting this scene—spotless hospital with daz-

zling white sheets and pillowcases on the beds—
with the filthy vermin-ridden barracks at Ravensbruck where she had last been present at a reli-
gious meeting. Here participation of the patients was
encouraged by the staff, it was all part of the therapy
to refresh them in mind and body. In the camp every
such gathering had been furtive, and voices were
kept as low as possible so as to escape the attention
of the guards.

"We've already looked after your traveling companion, Miss Prins," the smiling Superintendent told
Corrie as she sat in her room. "She's tucked up in bed
all clean and comfortable. Now, what can we do for
you?"

*Fancy meeting people who are so concerned
about my well-being*, thought Corrie. *What a contrast
to trying to keep out of the way of heartless and agres-
sive guards. I shall soon wake up and find I've been
dreaming after all. Kindness like this can't be real.*

But the lovely meal that was spread before Corrie in the dining room was no fantasy. It was good,
solid, wholesome food—the like of which she had
not seen for many a long day. Each bite seemed to
bring fresh strength into her poor, starved body.

The nurse who had taken her to the meal turned
out to be one of the YWCA leaders from Haarlem. It
didn't take Corrie long to recognize her, but no wonder Truus couldn't believe she had met up with Corrie ten Boom again. It couldn't be!

Corrie felt a little puzzled at this lack of recogni-
tion, until for the first time in a year she caught sight
of herself in a long mirror. Perhaps she could excuse
Truus after all! Admittedly, Corrie had never been

very interested in clothes, but with Betsie's kindly supervision she had usually gone out clean and tidy to her various meetings and activities.

Now she looked like a scarecrow with her pale thin face, filthy ill-fitting clothes and straggly, greasy hair. It was hardly surprising that even a close friend had failed to recognize her.

The next most important item on her program was a bath. Again and again Corrie let the warm, refreshing water lap over her body. She could hardly bear to step out of the tub and dry herself, it had been such a blissful experience.

And then—even more luxuries! Clean, warm, well-fitting clothes were supplied by the nurses. No more thin cotton dresses marked with the hateful Ravensbruck cross for her. Finally, a comfortable bed with sheets and blankets and, the final touch, an extra pillow placed thoughtfully under her swollen feet. *It's almost a shame to waste time going to sleep*, thought Corrie to herself. *I feel as though I must stay awake to enjoy it to the fullest.* Soon sleep overwhelmed her and Corrie resisted no longer. There would be other more wonderful days to follow.

At first Corrie felt confused with all the unaccustomed luxuries of life. She stayed at Groningen for ten days and almost had to relearn how to cope with knives and forks, as well as plates and glasses when she sat at the table for meals.

Happiness surrounded her. The first tears she shed after her release were tears of happiness caused by hearing a broadcast of a lovely Bach trio. "I'll never take beauty and color and harmony for granted again," she spoke to herself. "I never appreciated them sufficiently until they were snatched away from me.''

A final blessing was a visit to a church where Corrie was thrilled to be one of the worshiping congregation. She heard from the same Bible, and listened to the same message that she had preached herself in Ravensbruck but under entirely different circumstances.

As she grew stronger in body, so the wish in her heart became more intense to be reunited with her own family—at least those who remained. Travel was still banned in war-torn Holland, but Corrie was smuggled on to a food truck with headlights driving south.

Her answered knock at the door brought a strange mingling of joy and sorrow—joy at meeting Tine, Willem and some of the children, but sorrow at coming to terms with the fact that Willem was dying. How the family devoured every scrap of information about Betsie! She only wished they could supply her with news of Kik. Unfortunately, this tall, blond nephew was still missing after being deported to Germany. Willem's nursing home for the sick and elderly was partly staffed by young men who were working there in disguise, anxious to escape the forced labor conscription.

Corrie couldn't rest there for long either. Oh yes, it was good to spend time with Willem and his family again, but there were other even stronger tugs at Corrie's heartstrings. Haarlem must be the next port of call, combining a reunion with Nollie and a chance to re-explore the Beje. How would it have

changed after her long absence and the German occupation?

She didn't have to wait long in spite of the gas
shortage. Somehow permission was obtained. On
the way to Haarlem, her companion, a man who had
worked with her very closely in the Resistance
movement, warned her of what changes she might
expect. Homeless families had been installed after
the bombing raids. Toos, the elderly female assistant,
had tried to reopen the watchshop in a small way.

Corrie scrambled out of the car as fast as she
could. The old familiar landmarks loomed in the distance, but she had eyes for none of these. Nollie
clasped her in a warm embrace and Toos stood crying in the background. There were plenty of tears
even on such a happy day—tears of joy because of
Corrie's miraculous return, tears of sorrow because
Father and Betsie had been left behind.

Nollie had worked wonders on the Beje, polish-
ing and cleaning, but even she couldn't erase the
traces of alien visitors. A few of Corrie's personal
treasures were missing which she was never likely to
see again. Still, it was no good looking back on the
past; the future claimed Corrie and all her energies.
There was need, desperate, urgent need, in still-
occupied Holland. So Corrie wound up the antique
clocks and tried to take up the threads of life again.

For a while, Corrie spent every morning in the
shop, but afternoon found her exploring the old cob-
bled streets on her battered bicycle. One important
errand was to search for the family cat. Try as she
would, Corrie never caught sight of him again, although neighbors volunteered information about

feeding him for a while until he had disappeared without trace.

There was still something lacking in Corrie's life. True, it wasn't for want of occupation. The Rangers' Club was meeting again, glad to welcome back their founder. Empty rooms in the Beje were filling up with feeble-minded folk who had received no attention under the Nazi regime. With the little spare time at her disposal, Corrie attempted to work out a simple training program for them.

She even wondered if God would call her again to work with the Dutch underground people. However, a single chance to become involved showed her that there was no future in it for her. God had used her in the past in that way but she had lost her old skills. What was His will for the years that lay ahead?

She didn't have to wait long for an answer. One afternoon as she came back along the narrow street to her old home, she realized just what was lacking. Nothing so far, however much she tried, had given her satisfaction. It was Betsie herself she was missing most of all. Corrie accepted Betsie's death as a fact, no amount of grieving would bring her back. But there was something she could do for Betsie. Corrie would far rather have done it with Betsie by her side, but that was no longer possible.

"We must look after people, Corrie, surround them with love and with flowers, when the war is over." Betsie's dream would be Corrie's mission. How could Corrie ever have forgotten? But how could she ever set about this daunting task?

As usual, the beginnings of the new venture were humble and inauspicious for Corrie. With childlike faith, she began visiting groups in churches, homes and clubs trying to spread the truths that she and Betsie had learned at Ravensbruck and sharing her vision for a rehabilitation center.

One day a wealthy widow came up to Corrie at the close of her talk. "My mother used to call on your aunt and often told me about your charitable work as a family." *Good old Tante Jans!* thought Corrie. *How we used to hate keeping still and quiet when her important visitors were in the house!*

The lady went on. "One of my five sons, Jan, was taken away to Germany. I am convinced that he will come back safely, and for a thank offering I have to open my home for you to use for people whose lives have been shattered by the war. God has told me to do this."

After Jan's return, Corrie went to view the lovely mansion now at her disposal. For once, she was at a loss for words; the reality matched Betsie's vision in every detail—the wooden floors, the tall windows, the statues around the hall and the incredibly beautiful gardens. . . . It was just as if Betsie had already visited this place.

Before the work on the house was finished the Allies had retaken Holland. Proudly the congregation stood in the Grote Kerk to sing the "Wilhelmus," the Dutch national anthem, reminding Corrie of the day during the Occupation when nephew Peter had dared to do just that, and in consequence had been thrown into prison in Amsterdam by the Germans. The stirring notes echoed through the huge stone building, reminding many standing there of loved ones who would never give voice to it again.

Little by little the mansion was filled—first with Hollanders, scarred both mentally and physically by the Germans, and later by Dutch people who had suffered in Japanese internment camps in Indonesia.

Teach healing and forgiveness to enemies as much as she might, Corrie could not reconcile war victims to Dutch people who had collaborated with the enemy. They were a group apart, untouchables who had betrayed their own nation and fellow countrymen. It was impossible to house them together—the friction and the tension was too great—so these Dutch traitors were housed separately in the Beje.

Over the next few years, however, bridges were built and slowly advances were made. Often the therapy began in the gardens, just as Betsie had prophesied.

The greatest test was yet to come for Corrie. As more staff came forward, she was released to travel far afield to raise contributions for the home and preach the simple message of God's love shining radiant even in sin-murky Ravensbruck. Her travels took her all over Europe, and to the United States, but most of all to Germany, where there was the greatest need.

After a church service in Germany, a former S.S. guard from Ravensbruck came up to Corrie, his hand extended. "Thank you for your message. Isn't it wonderful that Jesus has washed my sins away!" he exclaimed.

For several moments Corrie's right hand remained limp by her side. She just couldn't bring herself to extend it, to shake his hand proffered in greeting. Hadn't he been the one who stood by mocking while she and Betsie with many others were forced to strip off their clothes before entering the shower room?

I can't do it, Lord. Don't ask me for this, it's too much. Hurtful, angry thoughts jostled inside her. Yet it was she who was demanding such an action from other casualties of war. "Forgive your enemies," she had urged them.

Then, help me, Lord, was her silent plea. *I can't do it on my own.* As she prayed, a power rushed along her arm and generated a warmth and forgiveness for the man who was even now eagerly shaking her hand. Once more, the Lord had enabled.

12

Final Ministry

During Corrie's long, post-war itinerant preaching ministry, there arose more than one occasion when she felt the time had come for her to settle down comfortably in one place. Yet on each occasion, another call for help came or there was another clear indication of the Lord's guidance, sending her off once more to some remote corner of the world, bearing the Gospel message of God's love and forgiveness.

It wasn't always easy to accept. The war years had taken their toll on Corrie's physical strength and resources. After one or two unhappy incidents, she decided never to appeal for money for her various charitable projects again. Often that meant God kept her waiting right until the last moment for the sum required for an air ticket. Even when she arrived in a strange country, she might not have accommodation fixed or any meetings arranged. But God always honored her faith and never let her down.

In her book, *Tramp for the Lord*, Corrie wrote

down many of her experiences as a record of her modern missionary journeys. From war-torn Vietnam to prisons in Africa, from Iron Curtain countries to Argentina, Corrie traveled thousands of miles, her possessions in a battered red suitcase.

When she had worked on her own for twelve years, she was joined by Conny, a lovely young Dutch woman, who became her secretary companion. Conny's friendship and fellowship in the Gospel were a great joy to Corrie—so much so that Corrie was more shattered than delighted when Conny told her one day, "I've met someone who wants to marry me, we shall have to pray for a new partner for you."

Corrie felt ashamed of her reaction later when the Lord provided another helper, Ellen de Kroon, a registered nurse. How could she ever have doubted the Lord? Together she and Ellen tackled the work assignments that came in and soon found that they made a very good team; they were in tune with each other.

Sometimes Ellen had to use a great deal of tact to suggest even slight alterations in their program. Do you remember the little Dutch girl who twisted and wriggled impatiently when the dressmaker arrived to give her a fitting for a new dress? Or how she quite willingly wore the ugliest hats and most out-of-date outfits procured by the very un-fashion conscious aunts so that her two sisters might be spared the humiliation of being seen in them by their friends?

This trait still persisted. Corrie's main objective was to take the Gospel to as many people as possible in the needy world. One day Ellen watched her as she addressed a conference of wives of international leaders. Corrie's cardigan was one shade of blue, her jumper another and her skirt still another! Oh dear! how could Ellen convince her?

Diplomatically, Ellen managed to persuade Corrie that she wasn't wasting money if she wore more attractive clothing. "After all, we are ambassadors of the King, so we should be suitably dressed to take His message around to different countries."

It wasn't that Corrie was stingy—far from it, and the money arriving from her books and speaking appearances was coming in rapidly. But she was anxious to spend as little as possible on herself, devoting nearly all of it to her charitable projects. For instance, she was financing an ex-concentration camp in Germany which had been taken over to rehouse refugees and war casualties.

In the end, Corrie was quite grateful to hand over many of the shopping chores to Ellen, who saw to it that Corrie was tastefully but not extravagantly attired.

Corrie's accounts of her experiences are refreshingly natural. Far from being elated and puffed up by her international reputation, she never failed to record the angry word spoken by her, the momentary lack of faith or the failure to understand another human being's problems. Happily, she lived close enough to the Lord to put the matter right immediately by confessing it and then asking forgiveness.

As time went on, Ellen, too, found someone to love and cherish her—Bob Stamps, the chaplain at Oral Roberts University. Corrie took this philosophically, aware that she would miss her companion of nine years, but glad for Ellen's future happiness.

Again the Lord provided a helper, Pamela Rosewell, an English girl.

Although Corrie was unable to be present at Bob and Ellen's wedding in Holland, she arrived by plane at an airport in Oklahoma a couple of years later for the dedication and baptismal service of Peter John, their baby son.

February 28 was always a red letter day on Corrie's calendar. On that day in 1944 she was taken to prison by the Gestapo. Exactly thirty-three years later she moved into her own house, Shalom, in California. She called it "Shalom" because that is the Hebrew word for peace.

How thankful Corrie was to have a permanent place of her own again! At eighty-five, she was beginning to find long flights of steps difficult, and she tired more easily on her journeys. Soon after settling down at Shalom, she had a pacemaker fitted in her heart.

Even then, Corrie never visualized complete retirement from the Lord's service. She chose the United States for her home because in it there were many more possibilities of reaching people with the Gospel, many different channels of communication.

Following the success of the film, "The Hiding Place," based on Corrie's own war-time experiences, Corrie saw the possibility in spreading the Gospel by means of tapes, slides, films and television. In her new house she worked closely with her office staff, creating fresh messages and different methods of passing on the Christian story. She enjoyed being a hostess, entertaining guests in her own house, and she reveled in her beautiful garden stocked with shrubs and flowers from well-wishers all over the country.

In her book *A Tramp Finds a Home*, Corrie admitted, "My times are in God's hands . . . after the pacemaker was fitted I was glad and sad at the same time. I would have preferred to have gone to heaven, but I can spend an eternity there, and there is still so much to do here. As Paul says in his letter to the Philippian church, 'For me to live is Christ, and to die is gain.' "

On April 15th, 1983, Corrie passed away peacefully into the presence of her Lord. Even the date held a special significance for her as it was her birthday, exactly ninety-one years after she had first arrived into the world. This "poor little thing," this "very weak little baby" amazed everyone by her stamina, endurance and capacity for hard work right to the end of her long life, in spite of all she had suffered.

Although she has gone, the work which was so close to her heart will still be carried on. The Corrie ten Boom Missionary Memorial Fund will ensure that the missionaries with whom she was involved will continue to be supported in the future.

I like to think that Corrie's homegoing was much like that of Mr. Valiant-for-Truth in *The Pilgrim's Progress*.

When the last summons came for him, he said, "I am going to my Father's. My sword I give to him that shall succeed me in my pilgrimage . . . my marks and scars I carry with me, to be a witness for me that I have fought His battles who now will be my rewarder."

So he passed over, and all the trumpets sounded for him on the other side.